D0820775

Contents

▩ Volatile

PRODUCTS AND TECHNOLOGIES

Preface

Innovation in material technologies has been at the forefront of design discourse over the last decade. This emergence is the culmination of a widespread professional and academic recognition that knowledge of material properties and processes is fundamental to innovation in design applications, and further, that cross-fertilization among professional fields, as well as access to data outside of conventional territories, may broaden and advance the scope of landscape architecture. As a result of this material culture, conceptual and practical approaches to design development and dialogue have shifted toward a research-driven design process in which the opportunities and constraints of materials and construction techniques become integral to design intent.

In recent years, research and consulting services, material libraries, online databases, books, magazines, conferences, and exhibitions have surfaced worldwide to focus on new methods of collection, categorization, and dissemination of material data. Such forums of exchange have cultivated a widespread interest in the re-adaptation of materials for unprecedented applications: to be high-performance, to be environmentally efficient, and so on.

This new research model facilitates knowledge transfer among diverse professional and academic fields, and inspires a collaborative design process. A broader base of material understanding and design methodologies is now introduced at a much earlier stage of design development. However, along with this new model comes a necessity to formulate a new language to synthesize multiple field-specific terminologies, and translate them into relevant and comprehensible terms. Thus publications and databases have focused on the configuration of new categorization systems, and the merging of distinct terminology.

Within the context of this emergent material emphasis, Living Systems positions itself as a survey of contemporary approaches to material technologies in the field of landscape architecture. Despite a large number of both advanced theoretical essays and technological innovations in landscape architecture, theory and practice have not been synthesized in a single publication. Our research and publication therefore discusses landscape materiality within the context of diverse design case studies to illustrate how technology becomes integral to the conceptual framework.

Our editorial work has been primarily invested in both the assemblage of terminology to represent the expanded scope of contemporary thought and practice, as well as the invention of categorization to explicitly describe the dynamic qualities of landscape systems. More specifically, landscape materials and constructions are discussed first in terms of performance criteria and operations that facilitate and adapt to the cyclical processes of natural systems, notably: exchange, flow, metabolism, and growth; and second as interdependent systems, analogous to biological/natural systems (i.e. human body).

The book's categorization is derived from landscape operations rather than landscape products. For example, ecology, urban fabric, and spatial experience are described as choreographed events, so that landscape is understood as infrastructure, an emergent (evolving) organism, or a successional (sequential) episode.

Living Systems calls for a shift away from the traditional design process that initially identifies a landscape's behaviors and performance criteria, and then offers a range of product/construction solutions that can accommodate such functions, toward a design process which integrates the function into the design from the outset. While we do not propose to discard conventional categorization systems or material specification guidelines, we promote an expansion of terminology to acknowledge the dynamic performance of the medium, and comply with high-performance rating systems (i.e. LEED; Leadership in Energy and Environmental Design), which establish high standards for environmental, economic and social improvements.

Living Systems retools the current professional and pedagogic vocabulary, and is also intended as a gateway for other design professionals, including architects, urban planners, construction managers, restoration ecologists, and geographic computation analysts to expand their perception and expectations to reflect the new scope of the field. With an increased interest in landscape within architecture, we aim to deepen the understanding of the complexity and operative potential of landscapes as mutable, working systems.

In order to illustrate the diversity of the professional field of landscape architecture as it is discussed and practiced today, this book includes an eclectic range of topics, case studies, scales and contexts; it underlines the collaboration between landscape architecture, architecture, science and engineering, as well as the blurring of boundaries between the conventional professional divisions. Living Systems is intended as a portal to a broad directory of expertise, including design firms, research institutes, consultants, and manufacturers.

Projects are divided into seven chapters, each focused on an operative aspect of landscape. After formulating the thesis statement and chapter topics for Living Systems, an international call for project submissions was distributed. Over 60 projects were submitted, out of which 36 were selected to illustrate a range of conceptual and technical ideas. The enthusiastic response from design firms worldwide is a testament to relevance of landscape materials to current practice and dialogue. Each chapter presents multiple scales and properties within each operation in order to point to the operation's conceptual spectrum, and to inspire further expansion.

The project locations range internationally, featuring twelve countries, including the USA, Switzerland, Germany, Puerto Rico, Australia, Spain, Italy, The Netherlands, Denmark, The United Kingdom, Canada, and Greece. All projects are either built works in the last decade, newly built work within the last year, projects in design development, or conceptual proposals.

To complement the projects, a compendium of twenty-three material products and technologies are featured in the back of the book, and cross-referenced to the seven chapters and case studies. Some of the material technologies or experiments represent recent discoveries which often require new ways of construction and integration into projects. However, in many cases, materials are not necessarily new, but rather demonstrate new discussions, definitions, potential applications or combinations.

The book is formatted in a way to facilitate cross-referencing between operations and relevant material products; it attempts to promote cross-fertilization between materials and projects by categorizing according to function, operation, and performance. This format highlights systems and constructions that are designed to be multi-operational and applicable to several categories of performance; similarly, products are cross-referenced to multiple chapters to illustrate their capacity to perform multiple operations. Please note that all converted measurements have been rounded off and are approximate.

The index is conceived as a search tool for landscape processes and properties. Instead of listing architectonic forms and programs of use, such as plaza, playground, riverfront, or wetland, the index facilitates site analysis in terms of its properties.

The index is organized into two major systems: environmental forces which the design addresses (i.e. flow, growth, energy), and properties of material structures, such as reinforcing, tensile, and biodegradable.

Environmental forces are further divided into two levels of information. The first subcategory lists the active elements that harness the force, such as water, wind, vegetation, solar. The second subcategory lists the techniques to manipulate the active elements into potential design solutions. Those include terms such as retain, infiltrate, reinforce, inhibit, treat, and filter.

Introduction

In a recent issue of *Architecture Boston (AB)*, featuring the 2006 design awards, the jury's comments for the category of Unbuilt Architecture stated that the text in almost every architectural submission referred to its sustainable content, typically citing green roofs, geothermal wells, and reuse of rainwater, as if these were boxes to be checked. These allusions indicate a growing awareness that sustainable buildings and landscapes are desirable, but little grasp of how this may affect design. This aspect of architectural thought remains remarkably lacking in material association or in appreciation of the quantitative aspects of energy flows, rainwater volume, or natural light and ventilation.[1]

Among the projects awarded was an Energy Farm[2] where fields of suspended heliptropic sky-pins generate energy and activate variable intensities of light, color and sound; and a Fog Harvester, An Ecosystem for Arid Farmland Highway Stops[3], where a steel-mesh structure leverages fog and wind dispersal to capture soil, seeds, and moisture to launch and self-propagate a landscape.

Seeing such imaginative ideas increasingly surface within design dialogue reinforces the relevance and timing of the publication of Living Systems. However, that this discussion exists mainly within the awards category of unbuilt works is indicative that the interest in landscape architecture as an operational infrastructure is in its formative years: still open to a reshaping of concept and materialization.

Living Systems points precisely to the theoretical and technical discussions of such emerging interests, which include urban ecologies, remediation of degraded sites, stormwater management, energy generation, and climate control, among others. This publication addresses contemporary approaches to landscape material technologies and specifications, as well as quantification of landscape systems.

Living Systems redefines and expands the conventional boundaries of landscape materiality, both conceptually and professionally. It looks toward an intersection between the fields of landscape and architecture by blurring inside-outside relations and functions, as in climate control and water recycling; between landscape and engineering, as in the potential for landscape to prevent flooding, process sewage, or retain stormwater runoff; between landscape and urban-regional planning; and between landscape and ecological conservation/rehabilitation.

Living Systems, however, does not focus exclusively on environmental/ecological issues, which are undoubtedly some of the most commonly discussed design performance criteria today. Rather, it expands the concept of landscape materiality to also discuss its phenomenological immateriality, as in atmospheric, volatile, and phase-changing events. This publication also suggests the potential to merge digital media and data collection as part of the constructed landscape to communicate, monitor, and provide interactive experiences. Beyond quantitative aspects, these immaterial systems are examined for their poetic/symbolic performances, experiential/ethereal manifestation, or informative/didactic engagement.

Within Living Systems, the term "materiality" is defined according to four principles. The first recognizes landscape architecture as an outdoor space, or as a medium that employs living materials (plants, water) operating within the realm of natural/biological systems, subject to their complex behaviors.

The second principle imagines landscape as a motion picture film, rather than a static framed image; landscape material technologies are not considered objects, but rather processes that occur in varying scales, time/cycle intervals, and spatial manifestations. From day to night, from season to season, or from drought to flood,

1 Architecture Boston, January/February, Awards Issue, pp 92
2 Designer: Future Cities Lab, pp 94
3 Designer: Liminal Projects, pp 96

landscape is a stage for cyclical and evolving processes. Materiality is hence defined in terms of capabilities: growth, decay, exchange, conversion, adaptation, retention, infiltration, and evaporation.

The third principle argues that since these systems are in a constant state of flux, exchange, and transformation, they must be conceived as interdependent systems rather than viewed as individual material components. Consequently, material specifications must be considered integral to the design intent and structuring of the landscape, rather than specified as a superficial veneer to clad the surface.

The fourth principle debunks a conventional notion of nature as strictly naturally occurring, and instead points to the alliance between nature and technology. Regardless of its context, nature/landscape is a constructed system, impacted and adapted by technology within the contemporary built environment.

Living Systems presents 36 built and unbuilt projects that have been selected to demonstrate a range of strategies for the publication's conceptual principles and proposed categorization. The dissection of each project is a precise slice, or a section cut through a single highlighted material system. Material technologies are discussed within the context of design projects in order to demonstrate how the design principles outlined in each chapter can apply to a variety of site conditions and scales.

The classification and terminology generated through the course of the writing of this book describes processes and properties, which is a departure from the conventional categorization by predetermined applications. Material technologies and projects then are grouped according to function, not product typology. This paradigm shift in the design process is intended to inspire innovative material and construction solutions that go beyond the performance of typical ones.

The terminology is composed of verbs and adjectives that allude to the human/animal body and its complex life cycle. The terms are then cross-referenced within the chapters, product section, and index. The following seven chapter categories are not meant to be absolute, or exhaustive; they are merely a starting point for a new language of landscape definitions and terminology.

1. Launch investigates the rising interest in vertical landscapes, such as hanging gardens, tensile vine structures, and multi-tiered green façades. It also highlights a synthesis between landscape and architecture: for instance, where architectural façades are embedded with living materials to provide climate control. Launch capitalizes on the inherent plasticity of plants to adapt and redirect their growth. Much like a scaffolding structure for a building under construction, Launch points to an array of support structures that reinforce and guide the growth of the plants indefinitely, or until they reach stability. Both below-ground (i.e. geotextiles) and above-ground (i.e. tensile cables, trellis) structures are grouped together in order to imply a potential for a structural/formal continuity, and transcendence beyond typical placement. The structures featured in Launch can be transitional/biodegradable, permanent, or designed to evolve symbiotically, such as to adapt themselves to different stages of growth.

2. Stratify redefines the ground as a three-dimensional profile, and departs from the conventional separation between paving/surfaces and soil. Conceived as an epidermis-like structure, the stratified layers of the ground breathe, exchange nutrients, seal contaminants, drain/retain water, contain technological infrastructure, sustain vegetation, and provide structural support. Modular systems are examined for their capability to seamlessly transition between softscape and hardscape, and between biologically active and non-active. For example, a paving system may be constructed to function not only as a travel surface, but also as infrastructure that retains and distributes water in order to irrigate surrounding trees and plants.

3. Fluid focuses on landscape structures designed to flexibly accommodate the cyclical and seasonal fluctuations of water flow in terms of its volume, frequency and velocity. From drought to flood, and from erosion to the conveyance of pollutants, the structures and materials featured in this chapter retain, infiltrate, redirect/redistribute, control-release, or attenuate flows.

4. Grooming redefines preconceived notions of maintenance. It broadens the scope of maintenance beyond post-construction management and includes site preparation and construction process as part of a continuum of actions within an overall design intent. It is imagined as a series of choreographed performances throughout the lifecycle of a landscape site that have distinct visual and experiential forms.

5. Digestive examines the landscape as a metabolic system, where all materials and processes are inputs and outputs within a food cycle; they may be nutritious, innocuous, excessive, or harmful. Digestive features singular or ongoing processes that generate, retain, reshape, or biodegrade materials. Such processes may be physical, i.e. soil cut and fill, or bio-chemical, i.e. bioremediation via plants/fungus. Digestive promotes in-situ strategies for a zero waste approach, a departure from the conventional removal of pollutants or excess materials offsite to centralized systems, such as landfills, or sewage treatment plants.

6. Translate introduces the function of conversion which encompasses the interpretation of collected data into various onsite displays of communication, as well as the adaptation of energy forces (wind, solar, tidal, circulation motion) into new mechanical uses. Since energy dynamics are immaterial, and not usually quantifiable by park visitors, Translate features structures that endow these forces with a communicative visual language, or convert them into useful functions. The collected data may pertain to the site's environmental, political, socio-economic, or professional context. It may be obtained remotely, or from on-site sensors; it then becomes synthesized, decoded, evaluated, and translated into informative displays, such as signage, lighting, and sound, to name a few.

7. Volatile considers how weather dynamics can be conceived as a tectonic landscape experience. The premise for the chapter is to question how atmospheric phenomena and immaterial substances that lack a stable form, such as wind, rain, fog, clouds, light, and sound, can be technically constructed and specified. Technologies featured in Volatile may visually reframe familiar weather phenomena into new settings, or recreate artificially choreographed weather events. These technologies highlight the multiple-phase, auditory, optical and kinesthetic properties of weather over time. They reinforce the fleeting and ethereal processes that order the landscape on a macro scale and point to larger pervasive patterns that operate globally, but activate the immediate site.

Although the case study projects are categorized according to the chapters outlined above, many of the material technologies overlap in terms of functionality; this suggests a more fluid logic of connectivity between systems that generates multi-functionality. Several projects exemplify what architects Weiss/Manfredi call "zones of intensity", a stacking of operations at different scales and sequences that build upon one another to achieve an economy of means, an efficient use of resources, and an overall improved performance. The Fiber Optic Marsh project, for example, featured on the book's cover, combines a Launch system that provides a support structure for plants and habitat; a Fluid system that reinforces coastal erosion control; as well as a Translate system that senses and communicates water pollution levels through an illuminated nighttime fiber optic display.

■ Launch

WHILE CABLE FRAMEWORKS ARE NOT TYPICALLY GROUPED WITH SUBSOIL REINFORCEMENT SYSTEMS, LAUNCH PROPOSES THE POTENTIAL TO MERGE BOTH BELOW- AND ABOVE-GROUND SUPPORT STRUCTURES IN A VERTICAL CONTINUUM: A UNIFIED SYSTEM THAT CAN REINFORCE AND DIRECT THE DEVELOPMENT OF THE PLANTS' ENTIRE COMPOSITION.

The growth of plants, from initial planting to maturation, is characterized by a continuous gain in height, mass, and strength over time. The challenge often lies in the plant's infancy stage where its structural fragility requires external support in order to withstand wind and erosive forces. The concept of Launch is a combination of living and nonliving systems: a progression of vegetal growth and its correspondent structural scaffolding that is required to guide the plant's form and trajectory until it reaches stability.

The scaffold may be a transitional structure, i.e. biodegradable; permanent; or designed to evolve symbiotically. The material systems include above-ground structures, such as a tensile cable, a mesh, and beam frameworks that allow for plant attachment, as well as subsoil materials, such as geotextiles. While cable frameworks are not typically grouped with subsoil reinforcement systems, Launch proposes the potential to merge both below- and above-ground support structures in a vertical continuum: a unified system that can reinforce and direct the development of the plants' entire composition.

Although fragile, plants can also be invasive and consuming, grafting themselves fiercely onto any surface. MAK t6 VACANT takes advantage of this proclivity, and uses an architectural structure as a host consumed by a parasitic Strangler Fig. The project mimics the natural process of the Strangler Fig as it slowly envelops, fuses, and decimates a tree, to become a structurally independent organism in the hollow shape of its host. In MAK t6, the original architectural form acts as a template that directs the voracious growth of the Fig tree to form new ramp and platform structures.

Launch demonstrates a rising interest in vertical landscapes. Within the fields of landscape and architecture, this interest in typologies such as hanging gardens, tensile vine structures, and multi-tiered green façades emerges from the desire to expand the definition of landscape solely as a horizontal ground plane, and capitalizes on the inherent plasticity of plants to adapt and redirect their growth toward any supporting surface or source of nutrition, light, and water.

Vertical landscapes also represent a conceptual shift toward a synthesis between landscape and architecture; building façades, as an example, can be embedded within emergent, active, and responsive skins. The nonliving architectural structure may provide support for vegetal growth, elevated circulation, and opportunities to integrate irrigation, lighting, and technology. In turn, the emergent vegetal epidermis regulates the building's temperature, air quality, light transmission, and seasonal color.

MFO Park and the Fire-Escape Ecosystem both exemplify a multi-tiered park. Composed of a highly articulated matrix of cables, loggias, walkways, stairs, and irrigation, MFO Park launches columns of vines and living walls. The building skin is a living, mutable entity that changes color seasonally and thickens over time. The Fire-Escape adapts its framework to integrate planters and irrigation to create a living façade for the London tenement building. Both projects blur the distinction between architectural spaces and landscape to transform divergent characteristics into complementary performance.

VERTICAL LANDSCAPES ALSO REPRESENT A CONCEPTUAL SHIFT TOWARD A SYNTHESIS BETWEEN LANDSCAPE AND ARCHITECTURE; BUILDING FAÇADES, AS AN EXAMPLE, CAN BE EMBEDDED WITHIN EMERGENT, ACTIVE, AND RESPONSIVE SKINS.

Both Palio de Bougainvilleas and the pergola in Parque de Diagonal Mar respond to contextual site conditions. The tensile and torqued Palio de Bougainvilleas vine armature responds to the local meteorological conditions and creates a twisted hyperbolic surface in order to resist the hurricane-force winds endemic to Puerto Rico. The pergola in Parque de Diagonal Mar integrates irrigation and misting systems into its tubular structure, in order to irrigate the suspended planters and cool park visitors on a hot summer day. Experienced from below and viewed from a passing car, these elevated structures define a new landscape ground plane.

The material products featured in relation to Launch include vertical growth systems, tensile structures, and geotextiles. Earth Cinch, for example, proposes a departure from the conventional use of subsoil geotextiles. Designed as temporary and biodegradable green tapestries in abandoned urban areas, these modular earth- and seed-embedded textile structures can be installed onto building façades or roofs.

Flexible growth medium (FGM), bonded fiber matrix (BFM), and various biodegradable erosion control geotextiles are designed as transitional soil stabilization systems. Whether hydraulically sprayed or anchored with stakes to the ground, the fiber (and seed) matrixes biodegrade within a prescribed amount of time, as newly planted vegetation establish their roots and provide long-term erosion protection.

G-Sky and Naturaire® systems offer the ability to construct vertical plantscapes. Similar in structure, they combine a metal framework and a perforated nonwoven textile fabric into which plants are inserted to create a solid green wall. Additionally,

Naturaire® has been designed to filter indoor airborne contaminants through a specialized selection of plants that absorb or break down airborne chemicals. In terms of energy benefits, indoor air is cooled as it passes through the plants, and when distributed through the building's HVAC system, the cooled air can contribute to temperature regulation and conservation of cooling energy.

■ Multi-Tiered Vine Park //
Raderschall Landschaftsarchitekten AG + Burckhardt & Partner AG

MFO Park, Zurich, Switzerland

In MFO Park, the second of a series of four new parks planned for a major redevelopment area, Raderschall uses a complex open-air trellis to create a multi-tiered urban park. Referencing the neighborhood's industrial past, the steel cable tensile structure holds vegetation and park circulation in an architectonic form more than 100m (328ft) long and 17m (55.8ft) high. THROUGH AN ELABORATE NETWORK OF CABLES AND PLANTING TRENCHES, THE STRUCTURE EMPLOYS THE SIMPLE GROWING HABIT OF VINES TO CREATE A SERIES OF SPECTACULAR IMMERSIVE LIVING VOLUMES.

Two vegetal walls or skins envelope the interior and exterior perimeters of the steel matrix, defining the space of this unusual park. Situated between the vegetal skins, a circulation route of steel stairs and walkways allows access to the upper structure, which includes a sundeck and loggias. The wood-decked loggias are cantilevered internally, creating opportunities for viewing the central courtyard and for immersion within the filigree of vines and structure. Bounded by the vegetal structure, a courtyard of green glass aggregate contains seats, a fountain, and vine trellises shaped like inverted conical columns.

The vegetal skins are populated with multiple species of vines that grow upon the steel network of cables. The vine-growing nets are isolated from the main structure by about 50cm (20in) to prevent the vines from threatening the integrity of the structure. At the base, cables express the vine habit with radial bouquets extending upward, resulting in a form that both anticipates and abstracts naturalistic form. The form also consolidates the planting pits and creates more porous circulation on the ground plane.

To achieve a constant cover of foliage for the entire height of the 17m (55.8ft) structure, two strategies are employed. First, on the second level of the structure a series of trenches support a second tier of vines that are trained on a thinner network of cables. Secondly, vine varieties were chosen and distributed according to the height at which they grow and deploy foliage so that constant cover was achieved.

All together, 104 perennial vine varieties were chosen including vigorous woody vines, such as *Wisteria*, *Vitis*, *Ampelopsis*, and *Parthenocissus*. The symbiosis of structure and vegetation is reinforced by the assignment of a single species of vine to each vertical cable, such that the structure fades away, allowing the forms to be dominated by the dynamic character of the vines.

The vines are irrigated by a system that employs the site's internal watershed. The floor of the park is drained to the planting pits of the vines, which in turn are also drained to ensure that there is never standing water around the plants. The excess water that drains from the pits is collected in a cistern and then pumped to planting containers on the second level, ensuring that all plants on site benefit from the rain harvesting system. The cisterns also function to retain water on site during rain events and thus serve as a dry weather water source for site irrigation.

The cumulative load that the vines will eventually place on the structure is variable and difficult to calculate. Factors such as wind resistance, rate of growth, and structural integrity of woody vines create an ultimately unpredictable stress on the structure that prescribes a strategy of structural oversight. The structure will have to be periodically monitored to ensure that the skeletal structure is not overcome by the living system it is designed to support.

MFO Park's design hybridizes the dynamism of the vegetal medium with the scale and volumetric effect allowed by the matrix of steel cables. THE RESULTANT EFFECTS ARE MANY, BUT PERHAPS THE MOST DRAMATIC IS THE STRIKING TEMPORAL TRANSFORMATIONS THAT THE VEGETATED VOLUME EMBODIES AND WITHIN WHICH VISITORS ARE IMMERSED. With each seasonal cycle the structure shifts from a bare steel armature into a spectacular display of foliage and flowers. With each year, the vegetation consumes more of the skeletal steel structure, which slowly recedes into breathing, rustling, color-shifting and growing materiality.

■ **1** Two vegetal walls envelope the interior perimeter of the space and encase a steel staircase and walkways. **2** The east elevation demonstrates the relation between steel structures and vines.

1

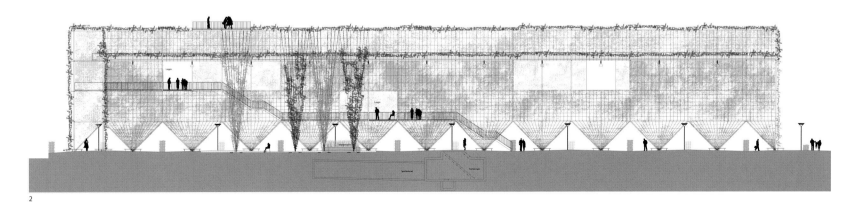

2

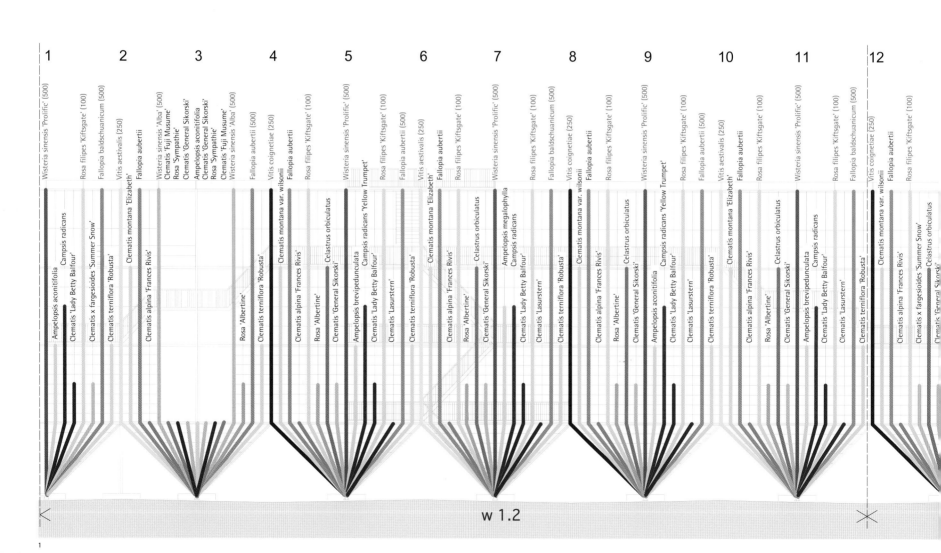

1 Vertical planting plan shows 104 selected vine species, each assigned to a separate cable.

w 1.2

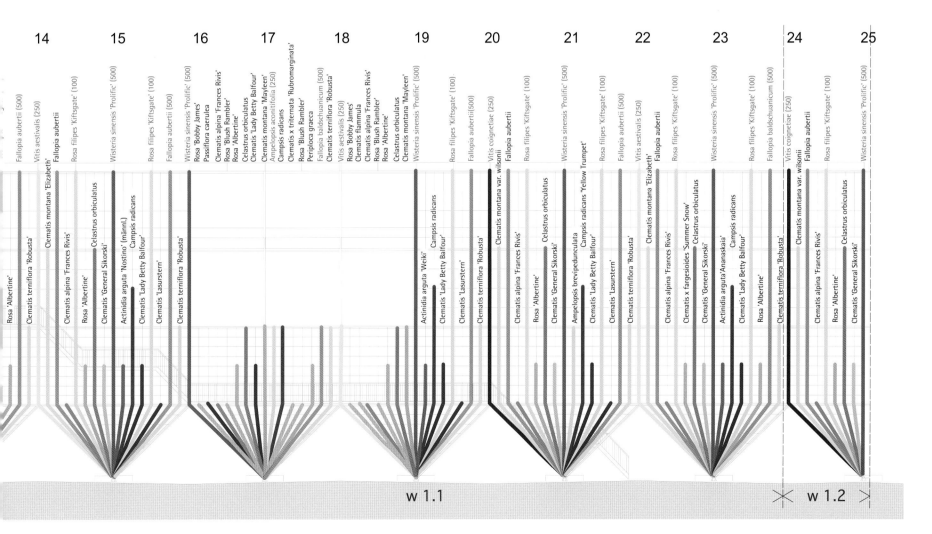

14

15

16

17

18

19

20

21

22

23

24

25

Fallopia aubertii (500)
Vitis aestivalis (250)
Clematis montana 'Elizabeth'
Fallopia aubertii
Rosa filipes 'Kiftsgate' (100)
Wisteria sinensis 'Prolific' (500)
Rosa filipes 'Kiftsgate' (100)
Fallopia aubertii (500)
Wisteria sinensis 'Prolific' (500)
Rosa 'Bobby James'
Passiflora caerulea
Clematis alpina 'Frances Rivis'
Rosa 'Blush Rambler'
Rosa 'Albertine'
Celastrus orbiculatus
Clematis 'Lady Betty Balfour'
Clematis montana 'Mayleen'
Ampelopsis aconitifolia (250)
Campsis radicans
Clematis x triternata 'Rubromarginata'
Rosa 'Blush Rambler'
Periploca graeca
Fallopia baldschuanicum (500)
Clematis terniflora 'Robusta'
Vitis aestivalis (250)
Rosa 'Bobby James'
Clematis flammula
Clematis alpina 'Frances Rivis'
Rosa 'Blush Rambler'
Rosa 'Albertine'
Celastrus orbiculatus
Clematis montana 'Mayleen'
Wisteria sinensis 'Prolific' (500)
Rosa filipes 'Kiftsgate' (100).
Fallopia aubertii(500)
Vitis coignetiae (250)
Fallopia aubertii
Rosa filipes 'Kiftsgate' (100)
Wisteria sinensis 'Prolific' (500)
Rosa filipes 'Kiftsgate' (100)
Fallopia aubertii (500)
Vitis aestivalis (250)
Clematis montana 'Elizabeth'
Fallopia aubertii
Rosa filipes 'Kiftsgate' (100)
Wisteria sinensis 'Prolific' (500)
Rosa filipes 'Kiftsgate' (100)
Fallopia baldschuanicum (500)
Vitis coignetiae (250)
Fallopia aubertii
Rosa filipes 'Kiftsgate' (100)
Wisteria sinensis 'Prolific' (500)

Rosa 'Albertine'
Clematis terniflora 'Robusta'
Clematis alpina 'Frances Rivis'
Rosa 'Albertine'
Celastrus orbiculatus
Clematis 'General Sikorski'
Actinidia arguta 'Nostino' (männl.)
Campsis radicans
Clematis 'Lady Betty Balfour'
Clematis 'Lasurstern'
Clematis terniflora 'Robusta'

Actinidia arguta 'Weiki'
Campsis radicans
Clematis 'Lady Betty Balfour'
Clematis 'Lasurstern'
Clematis terniflora 'Robusta'

Clematis montana var. wilsonii
Clematis alpina 'Frances Rivis'
Rosa 'Albertine'
Celastrus orbiculatus
Clematis 'General Sikorski'
Ampelopsis brevipedunculata
Campsis radicans 'Yellow Trumpet'
Clematis 'Lady Betty Balfour'
Clematis 'Lasurstern'
Clematis terniflora 'Robusta'

Clematis montana 'Elizabeth'
Clematis alpina 'Frances Rivis'
Clematis x fargesioides 'Summer Snow'
Clematis 'General Sikorski'
Celastrus orbiculatus
Actinidia arguta'Ananaskaia'
Campsis radicans
Clematis 'Lady Betty Balfour'
Rosa 'Albertine'
Clematis terniflora 'Robusta'

Clematis montana var. wilsonii
Clematis alpina 'Frances Rivis'
Rosa 'Albertine'
Celastrus orbiculatus
Clematis 'General Sikorski'

w 1.1

w 1.2

1

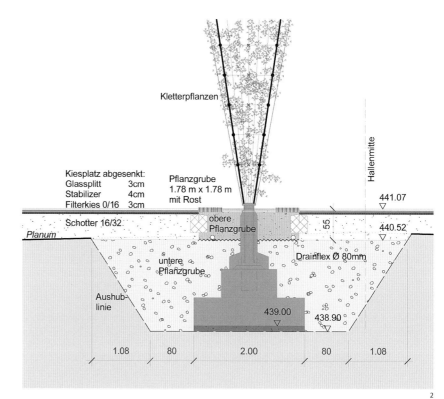

Kletterpflanzen

Kiesplatz abgesenkt:
Glassplitt   3cm
Stabilizer   4cm
Filterkies 0/16   3cm

Pflanzgrube
1.78 m x 1.78 m
mit Rost

Hallenmitte

441.07

Schotter 16/32

obere
Pflanzgrube

55

440.52

Planum

untere
Pflanzgrube

Drainflex Ø 80mm

Aushub-
linie

439.00

438.90

1.08   80   2.00   80   1.08

2

1 With each seasonal cycle the structure shifts from a bare steel armature into a spectacular display of foliage and flowers. **2** Detail sections of vine planting areas and structural foundation. **3** Detail of cable foundation. **4** Radial bouquets of tensile cables extend upward, allowing for porous circulation on the ground plane. **5** Detail of vine armature with a steel frame and tensile cables. **6** Circulation routes of steel stairs and walkways are situated between the vegetal walls.

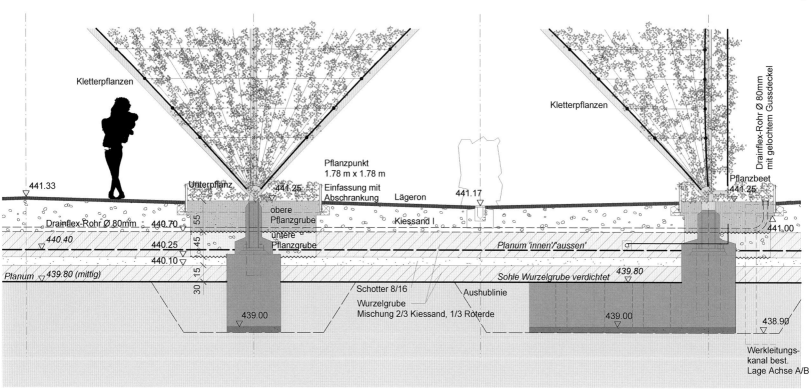

Kletterpflanzen

Kletterpflanzen

Drainflex-Rohr Ø 80mm
mit gelochtem Gussdeckel

441.33

Unterpflanz.

441.25

Pflanzpunkt
1.78 m x 1.78 m

Pflanzbeet

441.25

Einfassung mit
Abschrankung

Lägeron

441.17

Drainflex-Rohr Ø 80mm   440.70

55

obere
Pflanzgrube

Kiessand I

441.00

440.40

440.25

45

untere
Pflanzgrube

Planum 'innen'/'aussen'

440.10

15

439.00

Planum   439.80 (mittig)

30

Sohle Wurzelgrube verdichtet

439.80

Schotter 8/16
Wurzelgrube
Mischung 2/3 Kiessand, 1/3 Roterde

Aushublinie

439.00

438.90

Werkleitungs-
kanal best.
Lage Achse A/B

2

3

4

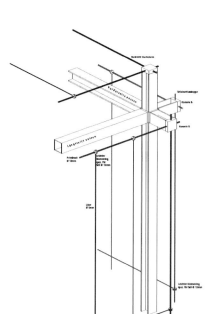

5

6

Misting Vine Pergola //
Enric Miralles Benedetta Tagliabue, EMBT Arquitectes Associates

Parque de Diagonal Mar, Barcelona, Spain

Parque de Diagonal Mar's pergola twists and turns ceaselessly across the park's variety of landscape conditions. To a casual visitor the shape resembles many things at once; a rampant vine, the trajectory of a bouncing ball, or the crooked lines of a twisted tree branch. This last form is consistent with the original idea for the park; it was conceived as a tree-like form branching from the sea, connecting the park with the sea and bringing natural forms into the city. These branch-like forms echo throughout the park as paths, pergolas, edging, and other linear elements. It is within the pergolas that this form takes flight, finding freedom to meander across land and water and define a variety of spaces and park skylines with their dramatic contours. IN ADDITION TO SUPPLEMENTING THE FORMAL EXPRES-SION OF THE PARK, THE TUBULAR PERGOLA ALSO SERVES TO COOL THE OUTDOOR SPACES AND PROVIDE SHADE. WHERE THE PERGO-LA FLIES OVERHEAD IN THE PLAZA, WIRES RUN BETWEEN INTER-SECTING PIECES TO SUPPORT VINES THAT GROW FROM ELEVATED VASES. The oversized vases are covered with ceramic pieces and float within the network of pergola forms, hanging like fruit from a vine. Where the forms intersect with pools, misters embedded into the pergola cool the air and mimic the atmosphere of the nearby ocean shorefront. Water for the misters, irrigation, and the park's pools is pumped from an underground aquifer that would otherwise threaten to flood an adjacent underground subway.

1

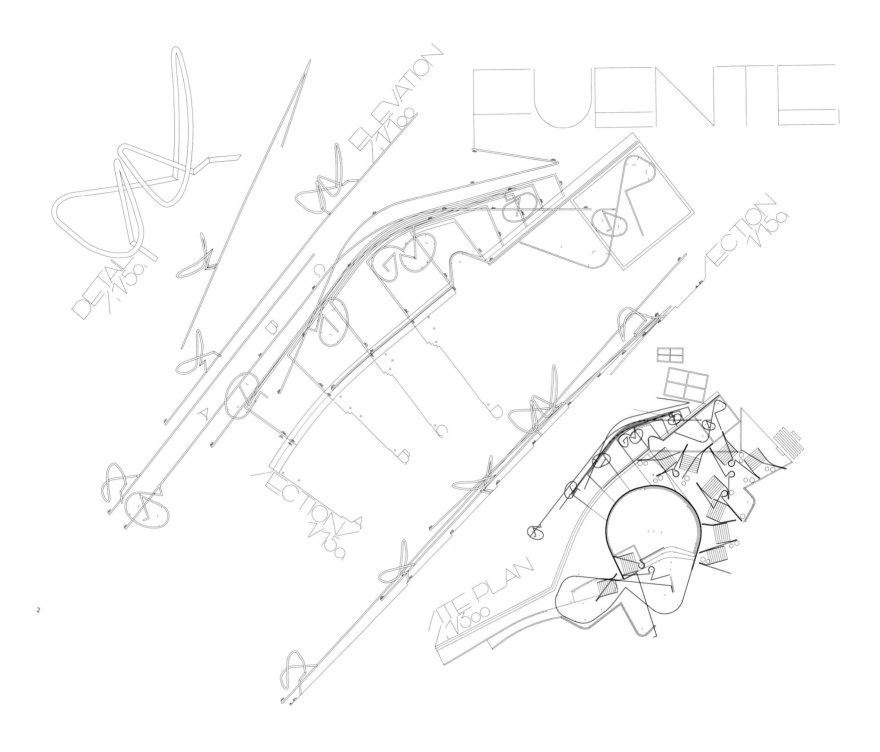

2

1 Misting pergola and vase planters with misters seen in the distance. **2** Site plan, sections, and elevation of pergola (reduced in scale).

1

1 Misters embedded in the pergola. **2** Vines grow out of suspended planters and climb the cable structure. **3** Reflection of anchored pergola in the pool. **4** Cables stretch between intersecting tubes.

2

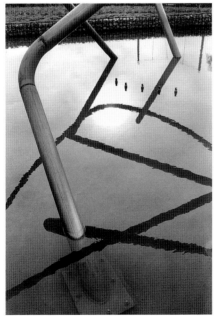

3

4

Wind Adapted Road Canopy Structure //
West 8

Palio de Bougainvilleas, Avenida Roosevelt, San Juan, Puerto Rico

Marching along a 350ft (106.7m) median, West 8's red-coated steel structure stretches its arms with vegetated steel cables, marking its presence within San Juan's busy Roosevelt Avenue. While this "Palio de Bougainvilleas" is intended to largely appear as an iconic "ecological logo" that responds to street conditions and cultural context, its structural morphology is also particularly suited for the local meteorological conditions.

THE CRISSCROSSING TENSIONED CABLES, UPON WHICH THE VINES CLIMB, FORM A MESH INCREMENTALLY TWISTED BY A SERIES OF TRELLIS ARMATURES. THIS CONFIGURATION OF CABLES CREATES

A TWISTED HYPERBOLIC SURFACE THAT PROVIDES THE SUPERIOR STABILITY REQUIRED TO WITHSTAND HURRICANE-FORCE WINDS. Additionally, by providing shade the trellis is responsive to both San Juan's hot summer climate and the region's frequent tropical storms.

In conjunction with its meteorological performance the hyperbolic surface provides supplemental visual effects. Viewed at vehicular speeds, the twisting armatures gel into an anthropomorphic animation of waving arms and undulating vectors. Additionally, the seemingly random mesh of cables enhances the filigree of vine shadows cast on the ground.

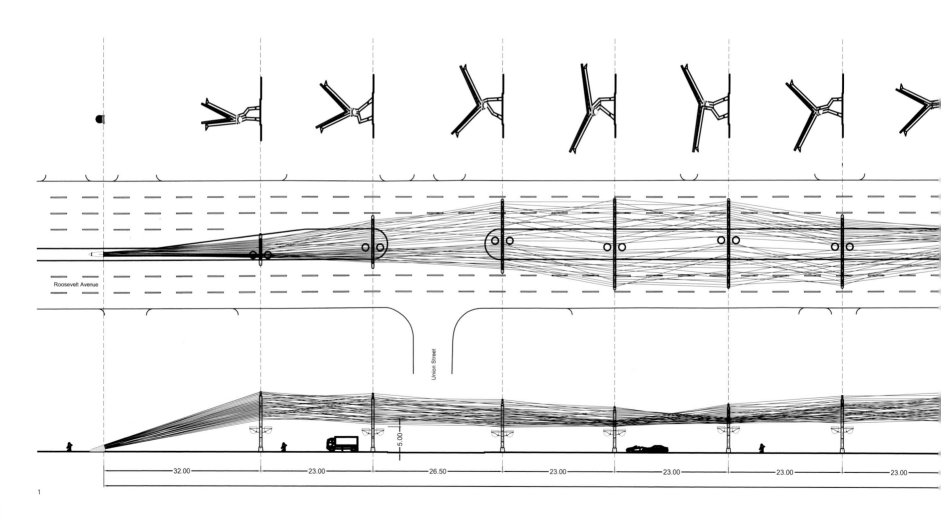

1

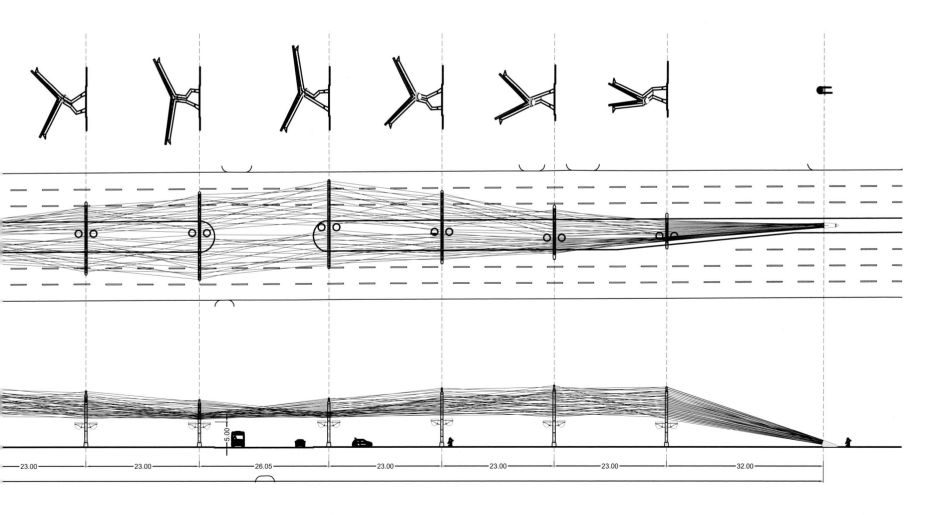

— 23.00 — — 23.00 — — 26.05 — — 23.00 — — 23.00 — — 23.00 — — 32.00 —

1 Sections of pergola structure with planters. **2** Viewed from the roadway, the twisting armatures gel into an anthropomorphic animation of waving arms and undulating vectors.

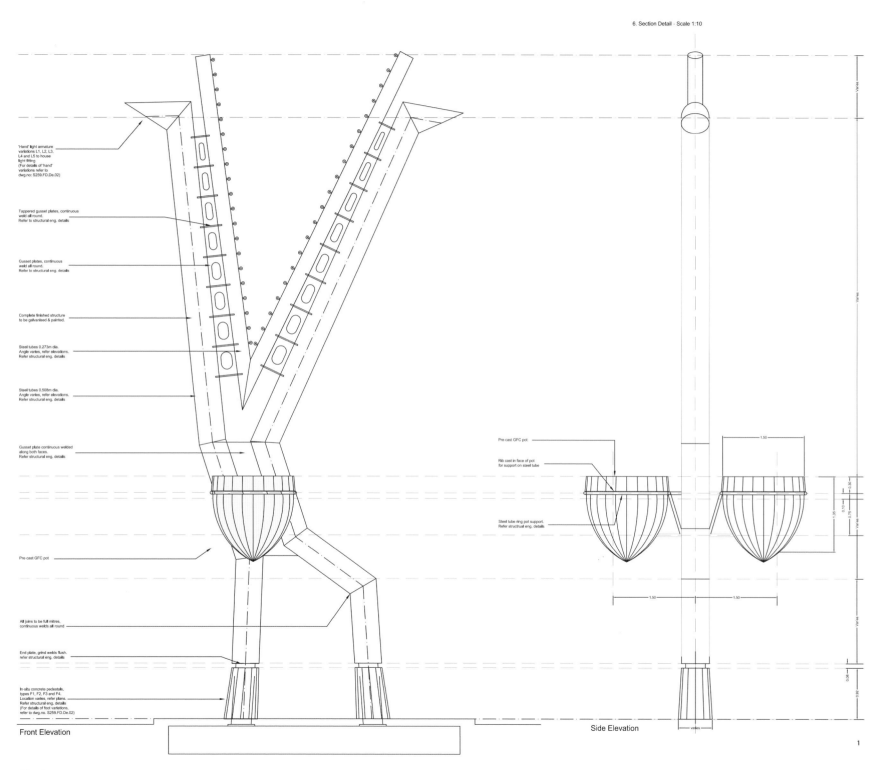

6. Section Detail · Scale 1:10

'Hand' light armature variations L1, L2, L3, L4 and L5 to house light fitting (For details of 'hand' variations refer to dwg.no: S259.FD.De.02)

Tappered gusset plates, continuous weld all round. Refer to structural eng. details

Gusset plates, continuous weld all round. Refer to structural eng. details

Complete finished structure to be galvanised & painted.

Steel tubes 0.273m dia. Angle varies, refer elevations. Refer structural eng. details

Steel tubes 0.508m dia. Angle varies, refer elevations. Refer structural eng. details

Gusset plate continuous welded along both faces. Refer structural eng. details

Pre-cast GFC pot

All joins to be full mitres, continuous welds all round

End plate, grind welds flush. refer structural eng. details

In-situ concrete pedestals, types F1, F2, F3 and F4. Location varies, refer plans. Refer structural eng. details (For details of foot variations, refer to dwg.no. S259.FD.De.02)

Front Elevation

Pre-cast GFC pot

Rib cast in face of pot for support on steel tube

Steel tube ring pot support. Refer structrual eng. details

Side Elevation

1

Fire-Escape Ecosystem //
GROSS.MAX + Mark Dion

GROSS.MAX and Mark Dion propose a "delirious Piranesi in bloom"; a vertical garden hanging from a salvaged fire escape installed along the wall of an 1890 London tenement. Planted with strata of native and exotic plants, this hanging garden launches an ecological gradient up the building's façade to reveal what GROSS.MAX refers to as the "artificiality of contemporary nature".

The salvaged fire escape is considered here both structurally and symbolically. AS A SCAFFOLDING FRAMEWORK, IT IS AN ORGANIZING STRUCTURE THAT CAN ACCOMMODATE A MODULAR PLANTING STRATEGY; ITS CROSSBEAM AND STAIR STRUCTURE ALLOWS FOR INSTALLATION AND ONGOING MAINTENANCE, AS WELL AS FUNCTIONING AS A SUPPORT FOR AN IRRIGATION SYSTEM. And as a symbol of London's cultural diversity, the suspended horizons visually extrude the building's floor layout onto its exterior façade and metaphorically express the diversity of its occupants as a lush spectacle.

Each stratum of planting displays different vegetation types and corresponding soil compositions. Plants are selected for their vigorous growth, cultural value and attractions to wildlife. They range from Butterfly Bush (*Buddleja davidii*) to London Rocket/Fire Weed (*Sisymbrium irio*) – a plant that thrives in building rubble and has survived many major disasters in London. A cultural reference to the local breweries is provided by Hop (*Humulus lupulus*), which is designed to wind up along the fire escape's structure. Other plant species represent the import of herbs and spices that were shipped into nearby docks in the times of the British trading empire. The soil mixes range from a sandy mix to heavy clay, representing the sedimentary banks of the meandering River Thames.

All plants are watered by means of a simple drip irrigation system and occasional spray irrigation via perforated pipes. Water regimes range from dry beds that require no irrigation, to water-circulated planters that boast aquatic wetland plants. Fine nozzles spray the lush planting of ferns and mosses; a micro-climate that is not unlike the famous fog of London itself. Occasional artefacts such as birdhouses and rain barrels focus interest within the overall structure.

While the fire escape scaffolding structure designates a particular planting gradient, its porosity allows water and wind to assist the migration of flora and fauna between the levels, thus creating an artificial platform for ecological diversity to achieve its own balance.

1

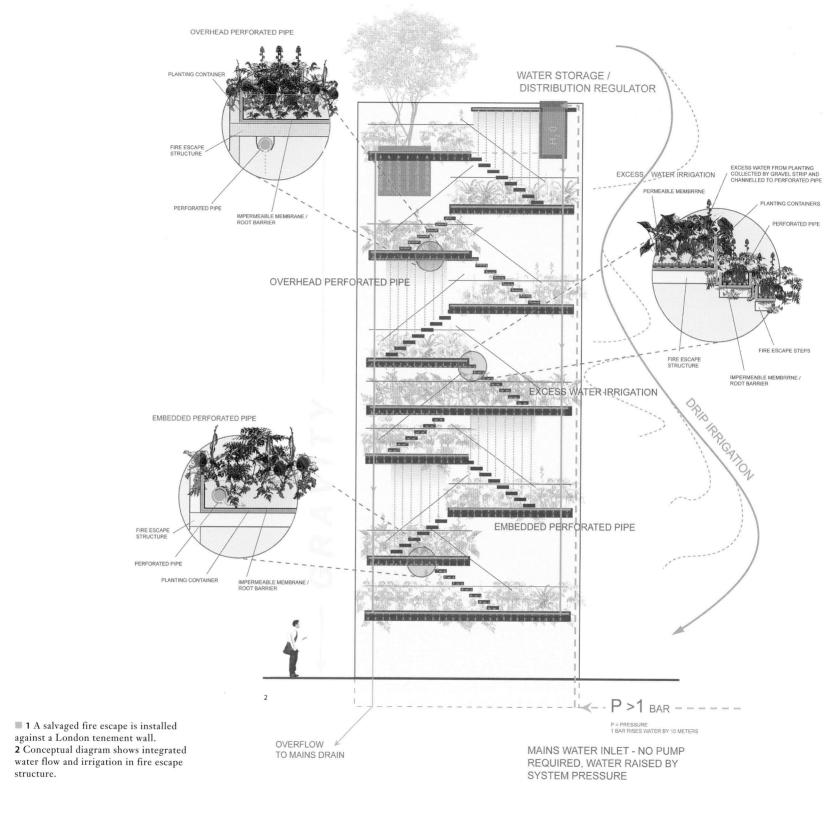

OVERHEAD PERFORATED PIPE

PLANTING CONTAINER

FIRE ESCAPE
STRUCTURE

PERFORATED PIPE

IMPERMEABLE MEMBRANE /
ROOT BARRIER

WATER STORAGE /
DISTRIBUTION REGULATOR

EXCESS WATER IRRIGATION

OVERHEAD PERFORATED PIPE

EMBEDDED PERFORATED PIPE

FIRE ESCAPE
STRUCTURE

PERFORATED PIPE

PLANTING CONTAINER

IMPERMEABLE MEMBRANE /
ROOT BARRIER

EXCESS WATER IRRIGATION

EMBEDDED PERFORATED PIPE

EXCESS WATER FROM PLANTING
COLLECTED BY GRAVEL STRIP AND
CHANNELLED TO PERFORATED PIPE

PERMEABLE MEMBRRNE

PLANTING CONTAINERS

PERFORATED PIPE

FIRE ESCAPE
STRUCTURE

FIRE ESCAPE STEPS

IMPERMEABLE MEMBRRNE /
ROOT BARRIER

DRIP IRRIGATION

GRAVITY

2

P >1 BAR

P = PRESSURE
1 BAR RISES WATER BY 10 METERS

OVERFLOW
TO MAINS DRAIN

MAINS WATER INLET - NO PUMP
REQUIRED, WATER RAISED BY
SYSTEM PRESSURE

1 A salvaged fire escape is installed
against a London tenement wall.
2 Conceptual diagram shows integrated
water flow and irrigation in fire escape
structure.

1

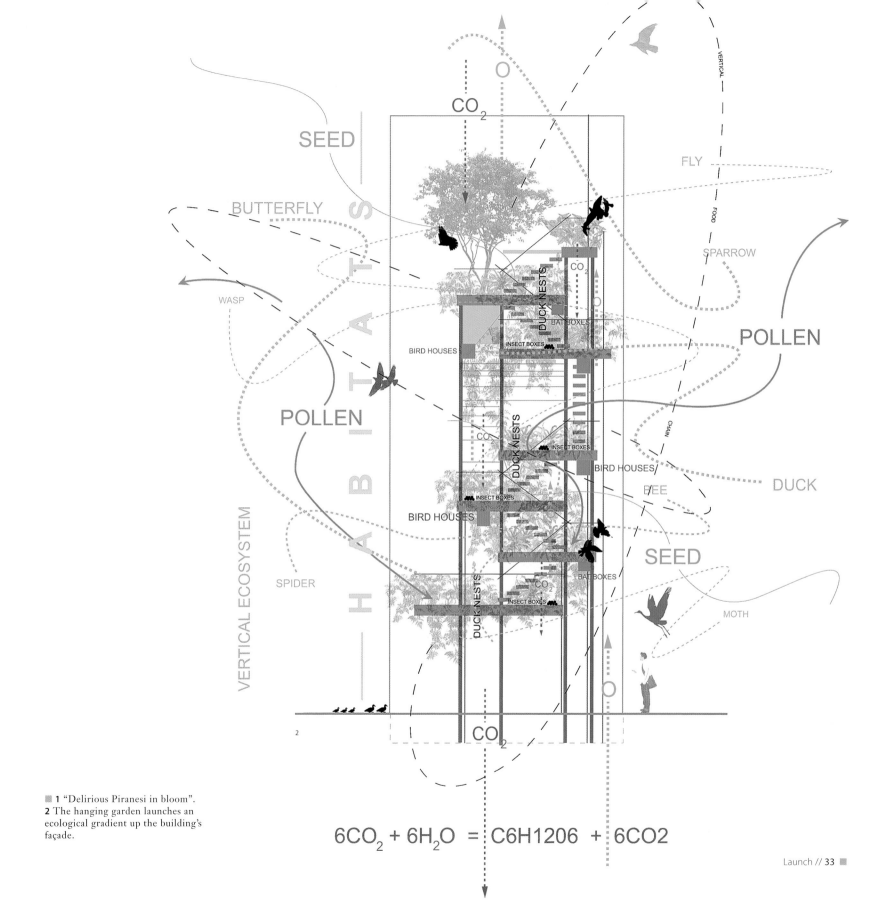

1 "Delirious Piranesi in bloom".
2 The hanging garden launches an ecological gradient up the building's façade.

$$6CO_2 + 6H_2O = C6H1206 + 6CO2$$

Parasitic Vegetal Structure //
David Fletcher + Juan Azulay

MAK t6 VACANT, The MAK Center and SCI-Arc, Los Angeles, California, USA

The genesis of a collaborative effort between a landscape architect and architect, the MAK t6 VACANT project asks the typical operations of each medium to both expand and concede. OVER THE COURSE OF MANY YEARS, THE ARCHITECTURE AND LIVING MATERIALS ARE ENVISIONED TO SWAP STRUCTURAL ROLES; THE ARCHITECTURE RECEDES, WHILE CONCEDING STRUCTURAL SUPPORT TO THE LIVING MATERIALS IT ORIGINALLY SUPPORTED.

The architecture is loosely based on the concept of cytoskeleton, a cellular scaffolding and dynamic structure that maintains cell shape and cellular components. Yet this project takes on a more macabre approach to the mutual relationship, as architecture becomes the host for a multitude of strangler fig vines that slowly consume it and assume their form and function, while creating a unique hybrid environment.

The project was proposed as part of an ideas competition by the MAK Center for Art & Architecture to explore how the center's preserved Schindler House could be buffered from "its increasingly vertical neighbors". The competition posits that the Schindler House is "inseparable from its gardens" and new "landscape dimensions" could mediate the imbalance of its new highrise neighbors. MAK t6 VACANT proposes two primary landscape dimensions as the vehicle for this buffering: resourc-

es and time. As a means to "rebuild the ground plane", opportunistic strangler fig – a vine that attaches itself to trees and will grow without direct interface with the ground – is hung from the top of a minimal wire scaffold containing a system of ramps and walkways. NURSED BY IRRIGATION SYSTEMS IN THE SCAFFOLD, THE FIGS HARNESS THE NATURAL RESOURCES OF THE HOUSE'S REMAINING DEVELOPMENTAL AIRSPACE, AND CREATE A HYBRID ABOVE-GROUND ROOT SYSTEM THAT SURROUNDS THE SCHINDLER HOUSE. The hybrid strangler fig/scaffold becomes a host for animals, visitors, and even residents.

MAK t6 VACANT is envisioned as a gradual process over a course of 30 years, where strangler figs will slowly grow to the ground, root, envelop the scaffold, and eventually gain structural autonomy when the individual vines fuse into a single organic mass. Fletcher + Azulay describe: "The vine eventually grafts itself to the inorganic structure, forming a compound organic/non-organic system that will collectively take on different characteristics and properties than either system can individually". This process, known as allofusion, will reinforce the existing architectural frame as a three-dimensional woven composite allowing for a new way to occupy the space.

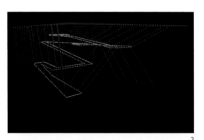

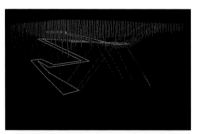

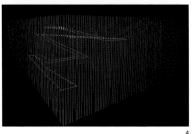

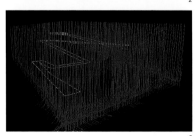

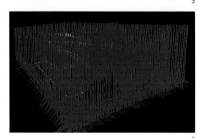

1 Initially, a tensile cable structure and ramps are built as a framework. **2** Seeding: Strangler Fig seeds are distributed across the top of the structure, mimicking its natural epiphytic germination process. **3** Sprouting: sending a network of aerial roots toward the ground in search of nutrients. **4** Grounding: tapping into ground level resources allows faster growth rate. **5** Buttressing: over time the roots grow into structural buttress formation. **6** VACANT: the dense aggregation of interwoven roots creates redundancy within the cytoskeleton and provides a new structural integrity. **7** The fibrous composite will continually increase its host's structural properties as it transforms it into an architectural jungle of vines.

7

Stratify

THE STRATIFIED GROUND IS CONCEIVED AS A THREE-DIMENSIONAL PROFILE, WITHIN WHICH LIVING AND DYNAMIC SYSTEMS - VEGETATION, FLOW, MICROBIAL ACTION - ORIGINATE, DEVELOP, FLOW THROUGH, OR ARE CONTAINED. ITS PROFILE EXTENDS BEYOND THE TOP/INTERFACE LAYER TO A SERIES OF OVERLAPPING HORIZONS THAT INTERCHANGE RESOURCES FOR REINFORCEMENT AND SYMBIOSIS.

In this chapter, the ground of contemporary landscape is reconsidered as an active agent and a medium of exchange: a singular system that can accommodate multiple processes and programs. Within this framework, Stratify investigates a departure from the concept of ground as an object or a noun (as in surface, paving, soil). Instead it posits ground as a verb, which proposes a series of operations that layer, composite, and aggregate living and nonliving elements to achieve a singular, unified and integrated system, characterized by interchanges and reciprocity between multiple components and properties. Rather than asking what it is, Stratify asks what it does.

Stratify re-examines a shift in the ground's material categorization from a traditional definition, such as surface or soil, to considering its ability to facilitate and accommodate dynamic processes. These processes are often composed of multiple, surging, and overlapping forces, including growth, physical flows, program elements, and weather cycles.

The projects featured in this chapter all fold multiple functions into a singular system, and allow issues like drainage, water retention or infiltration, vegetation, and structural load-bearing capacity to become integral to the design rather than add-on components. This approach results in designs that cannot be diluted or compromised due to budgetary constraints since the designs are generated with an inherent economic efficiency. As examples, The Maritime Youth House, Safe Zone, and Olympic Sculpture Park all employ single, yet complex systems to negotiate program, topography, contamination, stability, and drainage.

The stratified ground is conceived as a three-dimensional profile, within which living and dynamic systems - vegetation, flow, microbial action - originate, develop, flow through, or are contained. Its profile extends beyond the top/interface layer to a series of overlapping horizons that interchange resources for reinforcement and symbiosis. Within a composite system materials breathe, exchange nutrients, seal contaminants, facilitate drainage, retain and infiltrate water, contain technological infrastructure, sustain vegetation, provide structural support, and host multiple programs. Transitions between softscape and hardscape, between the shell and the flesh, between biologically active and nonactive elements become systematic, seamless, and "functionally graded" - a term borrowed from material science that describes composite structures with a gradual variation between different material compositions or properties, much like an epidermis.

Site becomes a critical aspect in determining the array of requirements and dynamic forces with which the ground has to contend. Within the context of the contemporary urban environment, the ground may not be the ground anymore, but instead be a cutout suspended in midair; on top of a capped landfill or a roof structure; or floating within a watercourse. Such sites give rise to design that expresses the sectionality of the stratified ground: design that exposes or implies the ground's layered construction, and design that demonstrates adaptations conducted by a single system as it adjusts to dynamic process forces.

The High Line project features an exploration of a modular system that can adapt to many uses and configurations. Built on top of an elevated, derelict freight-rail

■ SITE BECOMES A CRITICAL ASPECT IN DETERMINING THE ARRAY OF REQUIREMENTS AND DYNAMIC FORCES WITH WHICH THE GROUND HAS TO CONTEND. WITHIN THE CONTEXT OF THE CONTEMPORARY URBAN ENVIRONMENT, THE GROUND MAY NOT BE THE GROUND ANYMORE, BUT INSTEAD BE A CUTOUT SUSPENDED IN MIDAIR; ON TOP OF A CAPPED LANDFILL OR A ROOF STRUCTURE; OR FLOATING WITHIN A WATERCOURSE.

structure, pre-cast concrete planks mutate in their configuration to accommodate almost all of the park's operations in a single surfacing system. Integrated modules become paving, planters, drainage channels, and cantilevered benches. Elevated in the air, the sectional qualities of the planks are implied and further enhanced by the taut, seamless, modular design. Similarly, Wonder Holland floats a thin grass plane in a raised steel container to fit within the delicate ruins of its ancient archaeological site.

The stratified ground approach is relevant to projects featured in subsequent chapters, particularly chapters that concern flow and toxic soil remediation, as many constructed layers are designed to mitigate flow or conceal contaminants.

In the Fluid chapter, Blackstone Stormwater Garden features a composition of landforms whose soil profile facilitates both water retention and cleansing filtration. In Shop Creek's Drop Structure Suburban Stormwater System, soil cement has been added to reinforce the exterior soil strata to provide erosion control and energy dissipation for high flow velocity. At the Allianz Arena Munich Stadium, a surface gradient combined with surface porosity eliminates stormwater runoff through absorption, retention, and conveyance of water toward a rain garden, while integrating visitor circulation and vegetation growth.

Featured in the Digestive chapter, contaminated soil strata in Cultuurpark Westergasfabriek are coordinated with program and planting strategies, while at the

Urban Outfitters' Navy Yard Headquarters, the existing concrete surface was reconstituted to become a porous surface that would sustain plant growth.

The material technologies featured in the Products section of the book were selected for their qualities of soil retention, resilience, porosity, and reactive properties.

Land.Tiles are modular erosion control tiles that channel water and allow for growth. Structural Soils are load-bearing soils that accommodate heavy pedestrian traffic while supporting root development. Envirogrid is a three-dimensional cellular soil confinement that prevents erosion and accommodates heavy vehicular traffic, drainage and plant growth. Flexible growth medium (FGM) and bonded fiber matrix (BFM), as well as biodegradable erosion control geotextiles are applied onto the faces of slopes and stream banks as temporary erosion control, while allowing plant roots to penetrate the soil and establish a permanent slope reinforcement.

Soil Cement, a cement-modified soil, offers a rigid, structural and impermeable surface for horizontal and slope stabilization applications. Porous Concrete & Asphalt accommodates pedestrian and vehicular traffic as well as infiltration and runoff reduction. TXActive® is a photocatalytic cement that converts airborne pollution into innocuous elements. EnduraSafe™, recycled rubber mulch, provides a porous and resilient surface that also prevents weed growth.

Mechanically Stabilized Landform //
Weiss/Manfredi Architects

Running down a steep slope to a rocky shoreline, the site proposed for Seattle's Olympic Sculpture Park presented a variety of formidable constraints and opportunities. A railway and an arterial road divided the site into three isolated parcels, while the site's topography had been stripped by extensive soil cleanup and remediation. Finally, the shorefront seawall was failing and required repair.

The site was also suitably spectacular. Dropping 40ft (12m) from an urban neighborhood to the semi-industrialized edge of Elliott Bay, the site presented visitors with an array of far-reaching natural and urban vistas. On a clear day the snow-capped Olympic Mountains can be seen across a Puget Sound populated with ferries and giant cargo ships.

WEISS/MANFREDI'S DESIGN FOR THE PARK EMPLOYS A CONSTRUCTED TOPOGRAPHY AS AN ARMATURE TO NEGOTIATE AND ULTIMATELY CAPITALIZE ON THE SITE'S ARRAY OF CONDITIONS. Their zigzagging landform, which seamlessly crosses rail and road, unifies the site's topography, park program, and experience. To achieve a high level of performance from the singular structure, the landform has what Marion Weiss and Michael Manfredi call "chameleon sections". Each "section" explains how the landform performs within the park's multiple sectional complexities, while maintaining a unified form and surface. This "chameleon" quality was crucial to achieving a unity of experience and movement from the sculpture pavilion to the water's edge.

To achieve the advanced structural demands required to negotiate the slope and infrastructure, the landform is constructed with a system of mechanically stabilized earth (MSE). The MSE allows for economical and seamless footings for the park's multiple spans. The ensuing series of topographic reactions, made possible by the employment of MSE, represents the majority of the park's "chameleon sections".

The MSE system consists of stacked steel baskets holding rock and gravel in place and anchored by alternating layers of engineered plastic fabric sheets and highly compacted soil. MECHANICALLY STABILIZED EARTH WAS CONSIDERED TO BE SAFER IN AN EARTHQUAKE THAN CONCRETE WALLS AND IS SIGNIFICANTLY LESS COSTLY THAN REINFORCED CONCRETE RETAINING WALLS, PILES OR PILING CAPS ASSOCIATED WITH TRADITIONAL RETAINING WALL CONSTRUCTION.

With the MSE construction reaching almost vertically up to 30ft (9.1m) above the road and train tracks, the voids left between the rocks of the exposed MSE could promote unwanted habitat causing the eventual degradation and structural instability of the system. As a response, a series of custom pre-cast concrete panels were incorporated to protect the exposed MSE construction, serving as a shell to the landform's critical surfaces, and simultaneously creating a guardrail where required. The overlapping construction of the pre-cast panels allows for controlled slippage during small seismic events, minimizing the risk of cracking or catastrophic failure. The panels also become a sculptural element, their overlapping plates responding to the speed of the intersecting traffic.

While it negotiates site conditions, the new Z-shaped landform also provides for a series of new distinct settings and sectional variations. Each setting is marked with its own unique environmental and planting characteristics. Additionally, landforms and plantings control, collect, and cleanse storm water as it moves through the site before being discharged into Elliott Bay.

The landform also provides operational and creative infrastructure. Embedded in the path is a sub-surface system of water, power, and data, providing artists with additional resources for their installations. The sculpture pavilion and a garage are built into the top of the landform, completing the total unity of site, topography, and program.

The last in the series of the "chameleon sections" occurs where the landform descends into the water, serving as a tidal beach to provide new salmon habitat and to shore the damaged seawall. Here, the landform partially consumes the failing coastal bulkhead, pushing beyond to create a soft surface, upon which a variegated aquatic eco-system can develop.

Weiss/Manfredi's "chameleon sections" constitute a series of integrated responses to the constraints and opportunities presented by the varied and discontinuous site. Together, they create a reinforced landform that not only unites the site's topography, but also becomes an active agent in all the park's operations. The park, in turn, becomes a synthetic entity suitable for the cultural, urban, and ecological conditions it serves.

■ **1** The reinforced landform is a synthetic entity, suitable for the cultural, urban, and ecological conditions it serves. **2** Perspective/sections of the landform as it zigzags down a steep slope with switchbacks across rail and road. **3** "Chameleon sections" negotiating slope, highway, and rail infrastructure.

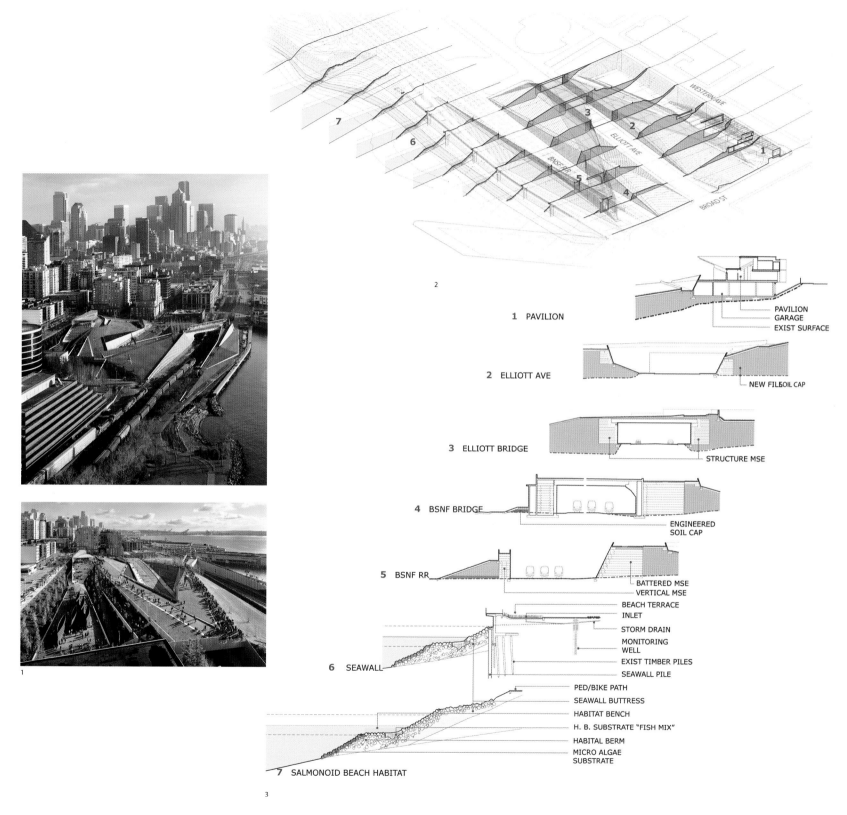

1   PAVILION

2   ELLIOTT AVE

3   ELLIOTT BRIDGE

4   BSNF BRIDGE

5   BSNF RR

6   SEAWALL

7   SALMONOID BEACH HABITAT

PAVILION
GARAGE
EXIST SURFACE

NEW FILL SOIL CAP

STRUCTURE MSE

ENGINEERED SOIL CAP

BATTERED MSE
VERTICAL MSE
BEACH TERRACE
INLET
STORM DRAIN
MONITORING WELL
EXIST TIMBER PILES
SEAWALL PILE
PED/BIKE PATH
SEAWALL BUTTRESS
HABITAT BENCH
H. B. SUBSTRATE "FISH MIX"
HABITAL BERM
MICRO ALGAE SUBSTRATE

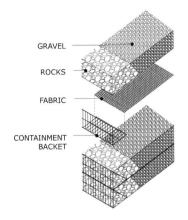

GRAVEL

ROCKS

FABRIC

CONTAINMENT
BACKET

MECHANICALLY STABILIZED EARTH (MSE)

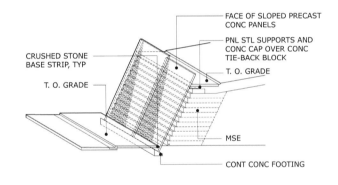

FACE OF SLOPED PRECAST
CONC PANELS

PNL STL SUPPORTS AND
CONC CAP OVER CONC
TIE-BACK BLOCK

CRUSHED STONE
BASE STRIP, TYP

T. O. GRADE

T. O. GRADE

MSE

CONT CONC FOOTING

MECHANICALLY STABILIZED EARTH (MSE) WALL

4"-8" QUARRY SPALLS
TO FILL VOIDS

HABITAT
BENCH

MHHT

VARIES 1

6' VARIES

EL. -3'-0"
EL. -6'-0"

MLLT

ROCK RIP-RAP
2.5' MEAN DIA

2
1

5' MIN

KELP/MICROALGAE
SUBSTRATE 2' DEEP

EXIST MUDLINE

HABITAT SUBSTRATE
"FISH MIX"

SALMONOID BEACH HABITAT

1

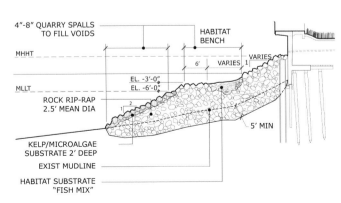

▧ **1** The landform consists of a series of "chameleon sections" that treat a variety of site and programmatic conditions.

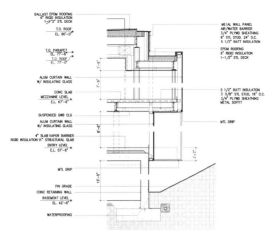

BALLAST EPDM ROOFING
6" RIGID INSULATION
1-3/2" STL DECK
T.O. ROOF
EL. 80'-0"

T.O. PARAPET
EL. 77'-6"
T.O. ROOF
EL. 77'-0"

ALUM CURTAIN WALL
W/ INSULATING GLASS

CONC SLAB
MEZZANINE LEVEL
EL. 67'-6"

SUSPENDED GWB CLG
ALUM CURTAIN WALL
W/ INSULATING GLASS

4" SLAB VAPOR BARRIER
RIGID INSULATION 11" STRUCTURAL SLAB
ENTRY LEVEL
EL. 57'-6"

MTL DRIP

FIN GRADE
CONC RETAINING WALL
BASEMENT LEVEL
EL. 42'-6"

WATERPROOFING

METAL WALL PANEL
AIR/WATER BARRIER
3/4" PLYWD SHEATHING
6" STL STUD, 24" O.C.
5 1/2" BATT INSULATION

EPDM ROOFING
6" RIGID INSULATION
1-1/2" STL DECK

5 1/2" BATT INSULATION
3 5/8" STL STUD, 16" O.C.
3/4" PLYWD SHEATHING
METAL SOFFIT

MTL DRIP

PAVILION EXCAVATION

CLEARANCE B.O. BEAM
2" OFFSET
B.O. STL BEAM
COVER OPENING BTWN
PANEL AND GRADE BEAM
W/ CONT 1/4" STL PLATES
STL SUPPORTS, SEE STRUC
VERTICAL PRECAST CONC
PANEL
CONC GRADE BEAM AT
ELLIOTT BRIDGE
FACE OF MSE

PROPERTY LINE

CRUSHED STONE
BASE STRIP, TYP
CONC SIDEWALK

CONT CONC FOOTING

GRANULAR FACE UNIT
ETI TG500 GEOTEXTILE
SUPPORT STRUT
TENSAR UNIAXIAL
STRUCTURAL GEOGRID
2"-4" FREEDRAINING STONE
REINFORCED GRANULAR FILL
DRAINAGE

STRUCTURAL MSE AT ELLIOTT BRIDGE

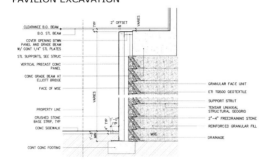

PRECAST DATUM
ADJACENT OVERLAPPING
PRECAST CONC PANEL
SLOPED PRECAST CONC PANEL
AREA DRAIN
T.O. GRADE, MATERIAL VARIES
CONC CAP, MIN 2"COLD MASTIC WP AT
EXPOSED STL CONNECTIONS
STL DECK, CUT
TO FIT STL SUPPORTS
TIE-BACK BLOCK

FACE OF MSE
T.O. GRADE,
MATERIAL VARIES

COLD MASTIC WATERPROOFING
OVER STEEL CONNECTIONS, TYP
CONT CONC FOOTING

BATTERED MSE AT ROAD AND TRAIN TRACK

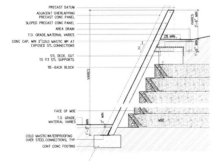

VERTICAL PRECAST CONC PANEL
ADJACENT OVERLAPPING
PRECAST CONC PANEL
T.O. GRADE
GRADE VARIES
STL DECK, CUT TO FIT STL
SUPPORTS, SEE STRUC

TIE-BACK BLOCK
FACE OF MSE

T.O. GRADE,
MATERIAL VARIES

CONT CONC FOOTING

VERTICAL MSE AT BNSF BRIDGE

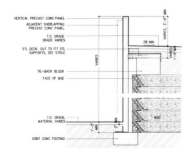

Floating Grass Plain //
West 8

To revitalize the ancient Mercati di Traiano, an archaeological site, is by itself a peculiar intervention. Furthermore, to attempt to build a landscape for the Dutch Embassy on the site, when the Supervisor of Roman Antiquities insists that none of the ruins be touched or damaged, seems a folly.

The design response by West 8 is appropriately unconventional. IT NEGOTIATES THE DELICATE RUINS BY FLOATING A GROUND PLANE AS AN IMAGINED "FLAT, VIRGIN CARPET OF FRESH DUTCH GREENNESS"

AMIDST OLD ROMAN RUINS. The structure is a simple raised steel container, planted with grass, and punctured like Leerdammer cheese with holes to allow for pieces of the ruins to protrude, visually linking and integrating the green carpet with the context, while also expressing its proposed connection to Dutch culture. The expression of this floating carpet is further accentuated by an outline of dramatic red lighting. Maintenance of the piece consists of watering and the "occasional attention of a lawn mower".

1 Floating a ground plane amidst Roman ruins. 2 Wonder Holland illuminated at night. 3 Maintenance of the piece consists of watering and the "occasional attention of a lawn mower". 4 Section of elevated grass plane.

1

2

3

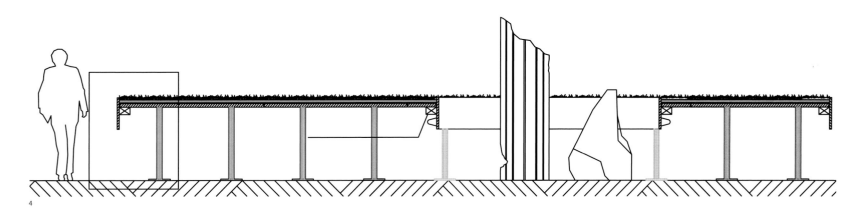

4

The transformation of the High Line, an abandoned elevated railway on the west side of Manhattan, into a new public open space necessitates a reconsideration of how a park operates. Given the constituents' desires to maintain the spirit of the existing vegetation now covering the fallow tracks, in combination with the programmatic and operational needs of a public park on a raised structure, the design strives to maintain the linear consistency of the High Line landscape while producing variation and a maximum of performative functions within a constrained space. At the core of the design, performing the most vital role, is the ground, composed as a synthetic surface that compresses multiple functions into a single system.

The logic of the planking, in 12ft (3.7m) long by 1ft (0.3m) wide modules, reinforces the linearity of the High Line and works with the direction of the rail tracks for easy reinstallation of long stretches of track and found objects. The long dimensions, differing from typical pavers, also invoke the industrial character of the High Line, works with the existing beams and structure. This paving system is designed as a single, continuous surface, yet built from individual units that transition from high use areas (100% hard) to vegetated biotopes (100% soft), with a variety of experiential gradients in-between. Gradual tapering of planks into planting beds forms a richly integrated and combed carpet. Pre-cast concrete was chosen for the planks for its durability, ease at making molds and forms, manufacturing replacements, controlling quality, and installation via a crane. The planking understructure consists of a series of knee walls at 6ft (1.8m) intervals that support the planks and keep the surface taut.

IN ORDER TO CREATE A SEAMLESS MULTI-OPERATIONAL SYNTHETIC SURFACE, THERE ARE TEN DIFFERENT PLANKING MODULES. Tapered units meet ADA, tripping, and trampling concerns by marking the edge of the path with only a subtle shift in geometry. In lieu of a surface drainage system, the entire planking system has ¼in (0.635cm) open joints for drainage, with sub-surface drainage mats that wick water into the planter beds. The paving system also integrates seating with precast units that flow seamlessly out from the system and create a cantilevered bench.

By placing multiple functions within a single synthetic surface the design gains many advantages, particularly suited to the unique conditions of the railway. Combining multiple functions into the planking system as well as integrating it into the planting areas creates a unified look and frees the park of the clutter that would accompany many disparate elements in a small space. BY UNIFYING THE MULTIPLE FUNCTIONS INTO THE GROUND, THE PARK'S INFRASTRUCTURE IS COMPRESSED, THUS CREATING MORE ROOM FOR ADDITIONAL PROGRAM AND VEGETATION AND ENABLING THE DESIRED "WILD LOOK".

1

2

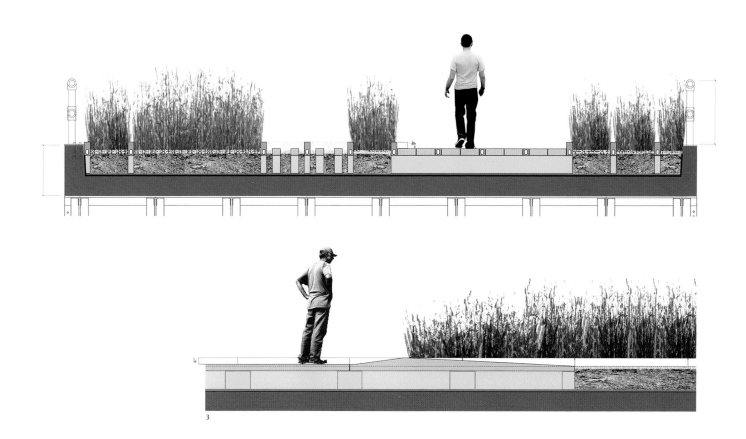

1 The multi-functional planking system integrates planting, irrigation, walking surfaces, and seating on a suspended rail structure. **2** Planking system model. **3** ¼in (0.6cm) open joints facilitate drainage, water retention, and irrigation. **4** Peel-up bench and grate plank detail sections.

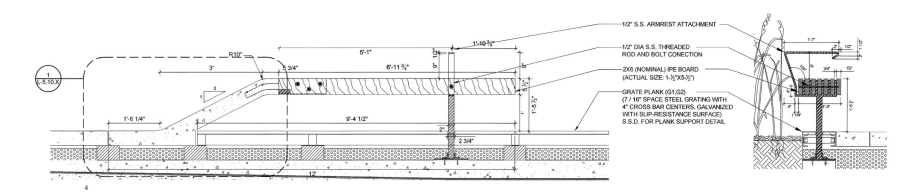

1/2" S.S. ARMREST ATTACHMENT

1/2" DIA S.S. THREADED ROD AND BOLT CONECTION

2X6 (NOMINAL) IPE BOARD (ACTUAL SIZE: 1-½"X5-½")

GRATE PLANK (G1,G2) (7 / 16" SPACE STEEL GRATING WITH 4" CROSS BAR CENTERS, GALVANIZED WITH SLIP-RESISTANCE SURFACE) S.S.D. FOR PLANK SUPPORT DETAIL

STRAIGHT PLANKS

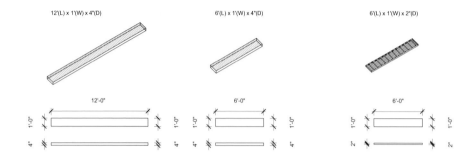

12'(L) x 1'(W) x 4"(D)

6'(L) x 1'(W) x 4"(D)

6'(L) x 1'(W) x 2"(D)

12'-0"
1'-0"
1'-0"
4"
4"

6'-0"
1'-0"
1'-0"
4"
4"

6'-0"
1'-0"
1'-0"
2"
2"

TAPERED PLANKS

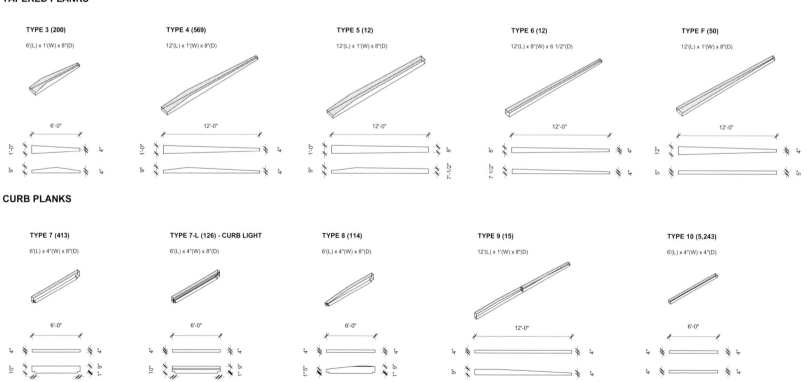

TYPE 3 (200)

6'(L) x 1'(W) x 8"(D)

TYPE 4 (569)

12'(L) x 1'(W) x 8"(D)

TYPE 5 (12)

12'(L) x 1'(W) x 8"(D)

TYPE 6 (12)

12'(L) x 8"(W) x 6 1/2"(D)

TYPE F (50)

12'(L) x 1'(W) x 8"(D)

CURB PLANKS

TYPE 7 (413)

6'(L) x 4"(W) x 8"(D)

TYPE 7-L (126) - CURB LIGHT

6'(L) x 4"(W) x 8"(D)

TYPE 8 (114)

6'(L) x 4"(W) x 8"(D)

TYPE 9 (15)

12'(L) x 1'(W) x 8"(D)

TYPE 10 (5,243)

6'(L) x 4"(W) x 4"(D)

1

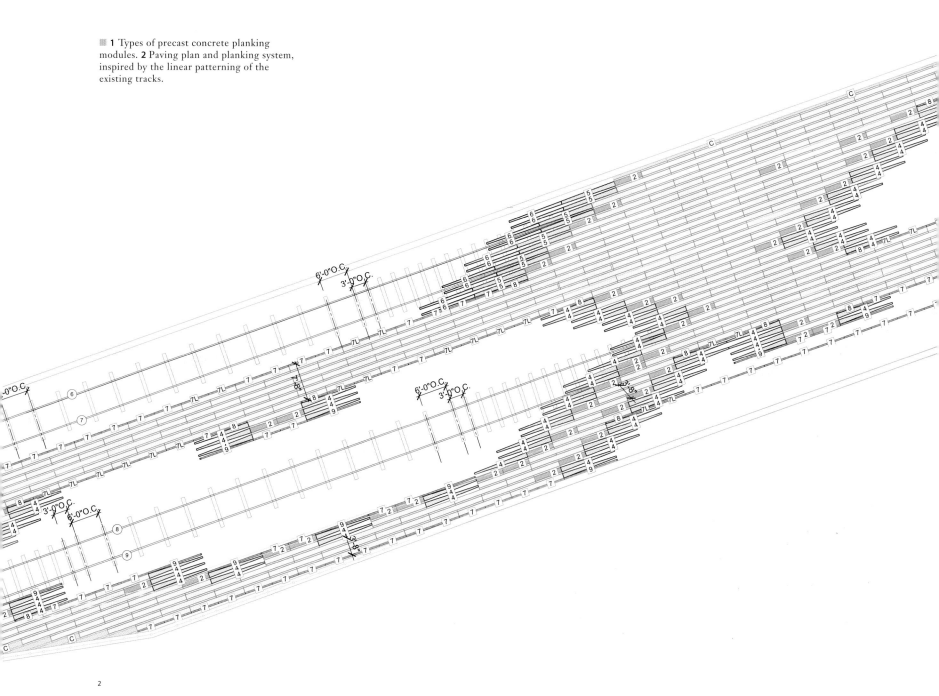

1 Types of precast concrete planking modules. 2 Paving plan and planking system, inspired by the linear patterning of the existing tracks.

2

Gradient of Resilience //
StoSS Landscape Urbanism

A synthetic rubber dermis grows out of forest leaf litter in the middle of the woods. CONSTRUCTED OF WHAT STOSS REFERS TO AS "LIQUID TOPOGRA-PHY", SEAMLESS STRATA OF RUBBER WERE POURED-IN-PLACE TO CREATE AN UNDULATING TERRAIN. The rubber layers vary in thickness and consequently in resilience, producing a gradient of elasticity and bounce.

The sub-base layer consists of local clay soils mixed with ¾in (1.9cm) angular aggregate as well as fine aggregate, then compacted into a series of 3:1 and 1:1 sloped landforms. Shredded Styrene-Butadiene Rubber (SBR) made of recycled tires and sneaker soles (0.25 – 3mm / ¹⁄₁₀₀ – ¹⁄₁₀ in granules) was then mixed with a Polyurethane binder (14% of the weight of rubber) in a mortar mixer and applied 1– 3in (2.5 –7.6cm) deep. The rubber was compressed with a roller and a trowel and trimmed along the edges. The cut edge served as formwork for the final pour – a mix of 1in (2.5cm) yellow Ethylene Propylene Diene Monomer (EPDM) granules (3mm granules) and recycled & shredded SBR tire treads (1– 3mm / ⁴⁄₁₀₀ – ¹⁄₁₀ in granules), bound with Polyurethane binder (22% of the weight of rubber). The valleys in between the landform mounds hold loose rubber mulch, "into which one could burrow or bounce". The rubber surface is permeable overall, allowing water to penetrate and infiltrate the soil beneath.

The thickness of the rubber constitutes the level of resilience. Typically, within the context of playground safety materials, the thickness is specified according to a ratio between the "critical fall heights" (from playground equipment) to the level of cushioning it provides. StoSS's Safe Zone uses this ratio as a point of departure to determine the thickness across the undulating terrain. WHAT IS CONVENTIONALLY A SINGLE AND FLAT RUBBER LAYER, ONTO WHICH KIDS BOUNCE, HERE HAS A VARIABLE THICKNESS ALONG ITS SECTION THAT CORRESPONDS TO THE TOPOGRAPHY. The rubber is draped on top of the undulating ground, such that a thinner layer is applied onto the peaks, as it thickens toward the base of the landform. As one runs across the "liquid topography", the variability of elastic qualities produces a surprising effect, as StoSS describes, "somewhat akin to climbing aboard a small, tippy boat, or jumping on a mattress".

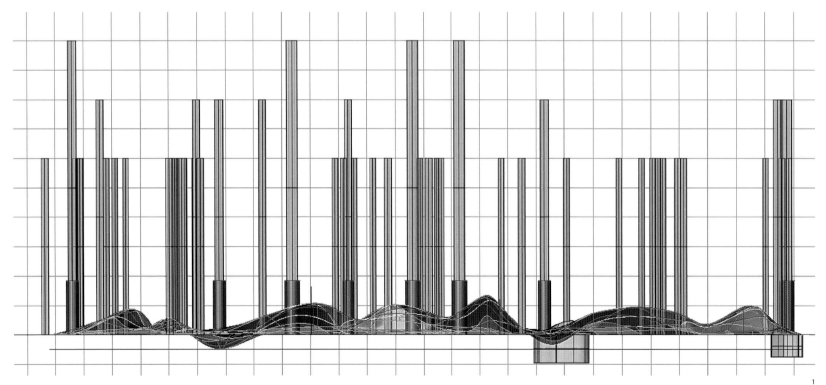

1

1 Elevation study of the terrain in relation to the existing trees.
2 The poured-in-place rubber surface grows out of forest leaf litter in the woods.

2

1 The rubber layers vary in thickness and consequently in resilience, producing a gradient of elasticity and bounce. **2** Detail section of the poured-in-place rubber topography. **3** Porous "rubber mulch" is used in low points to allow drainage.

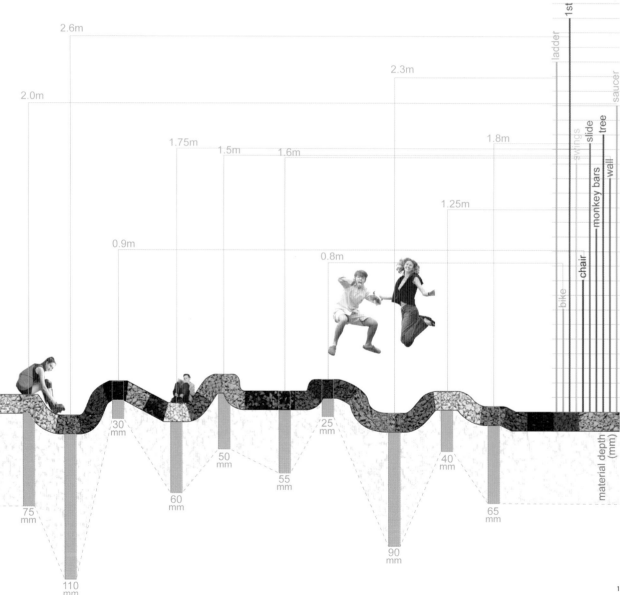

critical fall heights (0.1m)

2.6m

2.3m

2.0m

1.75m

1.5m

1.6m

1.8m

1.25m

0.9m

0.8m

ladder
1st floor
saucer
swings
slide
tree
monkey bars
wall
chair
bike

30 mm

50 mm

60 mm

25 mm

55 mm

40 mm

65 mm

75 mm

90 mm

110 mm

material depth (mm)

1

50

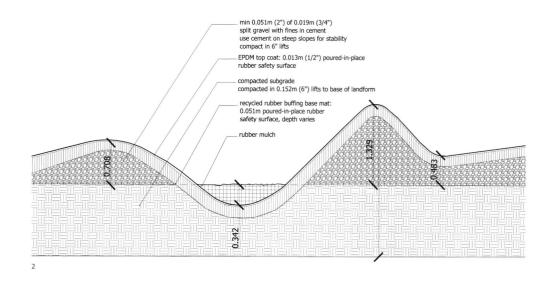

min 0.051m (2") of 0.019m (3/4")
split gravel with fines in cement
use cement on steep slopes for stability
compact in 6" lifts

EPDM top coat: 0.013m (1/2") poured-in-place
rubber safety surface

compacted subgrade
compacted in 0.152m (6") lifts to base of landform

recycled rubber buffing base mat:
0.051m poured-in-place rubber
safety surface, depth varies

rubber mulch

0.708

1.329

0.483

0.342

2

3

# Surface Inversion //
PLOT=BIG+JDS

Maritime Youth House, Sundby Harbour, Copenhagen, Denmark

A deck surface drapes over the site as a strategy to occupy the ground, while preventing contact with the contaminated soil condition of the site. With a rather conventional deck construction method, the surface is manipulated into a topographic and architectural expression and becomes both ground plane and roof. The deck lifts off the ground to envelop the building and then dips down to reach the harbour waters. CAREFUL ARTICULATION OF THE DECK'S VERTICES ALLOWS THE SURFACE TO PERFORM MULTIPLE PROGRAMMATIC OPERATIONS SIMULTANEOUSLY. WITHIN THE CONTEXT OF A SINGLE DAY THE DECK SERVES AS A ROOF, A RAMP, A STAIR, A GROUND, A SLIDE, A VIEWING PLATFORM, A PLAYGROUND, AND A BOAT LAUNCH.

With stipulations to clean the site's polluted soils and two clients the structure was required to negotiate multiple conditions and potentially conflicting programs. The Maritime Youth House specified an indoor sports room and an outdoor space for the kids to play, with special considerations for the pollution on site. The Sail Club required a large space for boat storage and a boat launch at the harbour's edge.

Soil decontamination would have consumed nearly a quarter of the overall budget. Therefore, the architects proposed an alternative solution: construct a wooden deck playground over the entire site (1600m²/17,222sf) and integrate buildings and boat storage under the deck, designating its upper side for recreational use. A grid of vertical posts varies the deck's heights according to programs above and below. The horizontal deck boards drape continuously to transition from one program to the other.

As the deck folds up, both its top and bottom surfaces reveal different conditions and mediate the conflicting needs to share inside/outside space. Rather than assigning programs to discrete areas, the singular materiality hosts a gradient of functionalities and programs, and endless opportunities for kids' play.

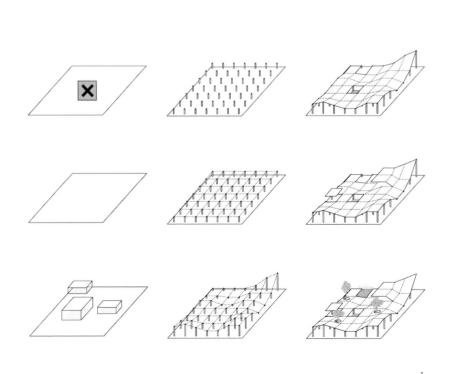

1

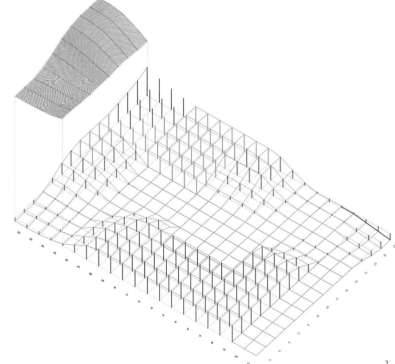

2

1 Relation of surface to site and program. 2 Three-dimensional framework of wooden vertices. 3 The deck serves as a roof, a ramp, a stair, a ground, a slide, a viewing platform, a playground, and a boat launch. 4 The Maritime Youth House specified an indoor sports room and an outdoor space for the kids to play.

3

4

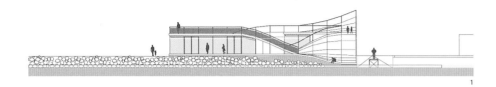

1

2

1 Sections: a wooden deck playground drapes over buildings and boat storage. **2** The deck lifts off the ground to envelop the building and then dips down to reach the harbour waters. **3** With a conventional deck construction method, the surface becomes both ground plane and roof.

1

3

Fluid

FLUID PERTAINS TO LANDSCAPE STRUCTURES DESIGNED TO FLEXIBLY ACCOMMODATE THE CYCLICAL AND SEASONAL FLUCTUATIONS OF WATER FLOW, AS WELL AS THE MANAGEMENT OF WATER VOLUME, FREQUENCY, AND VELOCITY.

Water is equally a life sustaining and an erosive force. Subject to weather cycles, with seasonal variations ranging from rains to hurricane, and from drought to floods, water flow is unpredictable.

Fluid pertains to landscape structures designed to flexibly accommodate the cyclical and seasonal fluctuations of water flow, as well as the management of water volume, frequency, and velocity. In this chapter, structures and materials are discussed in terms of their capabilities to retain, infiltrate, control-release, and attenuate flows in order to prevent soil erosion, conveyance of pollutants, or flooding. Conversely, the capture and conveyance of water flow is examined in terms of the potential to create habitat, as well as recreational and visual amenities.

Within Living Systems, water as a resource, a medium, and a fluid relates to every chapter topic: Stratify regulates permeability; Digestive biodegrades water pollutants; Translate monitors pollution or storm surges; and Volatile displays water's ephemeral phases, such as mist and fog.

In this chapter, all of the projects featured are associated with peak flows during storm events. However, each exemplifies a different type of flow dynamic ranging from large water bodies to small streams, from linear river flow to surface flow in urban areas. The projects demonstrate different site conditions and different scales: from urban to coastal riparian, from small lots to entire river sections.

Within urban and suburban environments, landscape is typically engineered to convey water rapidly away from built structures to prevent interior flooding and to clear exterior circulation surfaces. Current design, planning and policy regard the dynamic of flows differently due to several major concerns. One concern is the conveyance of polluted surface runoff into water bodies, which necessitates onsite retention and filtration systems. While many sites comply with such municipal requirements, its landscape form is not always integrated as a design intent.

The urban projects featured here demonstrate a retrofit design to inhabit the existing, dimensionally constrained urban fabric and infrastructure, as with Blackstone Stormwater Garden and SW 12th Avenue Green Street Project. The former is composed of a series of bio-swales that are designed to detain a 3-month storm event for 72 hours, consequently capturing and cleansing 90% of annual rainfall, and preventing polluted runoff from entering the nearby river. The latter features a stormwater collection and retention system that has been integrated into the existing sidewalk section. Distributed along the length of the street, the networked containers collect 60% of annual rainfall, and still accommodate circulation and vegetation. Such interventions, if deployed throughout the urban-suburban environment, can have a tremendously positive impact on water quality and flood prevention. Combined with Digestive operations and technologies, such as the newspaper nitrate treatment bioretention medium, researched by Allen P. Davis, the capacity for biofiltration can be highly efficient.

WITH A MAJORITY OF SURFACES IN THE BUILT ENVIRONMENT BEING IMPERVIOUS, THESE METHODS OF SMALL-SCALE, LOCAL WATER RETENTION, AND INFILTRATION BEGIN TO COMPENSATE FOR THE DEPLETION OF THE NATURAL SPONGE STRUCTURES (SOIL, WETLANDS) THAT WERE ONCE WIDELY DISPERSED TO ATTENUATE THE VOLUME OF SURGES, AS WELL AS FACILITATE GROUND WATER RECHARGE.

With a majority of surfaces in the built environment being impervious, these methods of small-scale, local water retention, and infiltration begin to compensate for the depletion of the natural sponge structures (soil, wetlands) that were once widely dispersed to attenuate the volume of surges, as well as facilitate ground water recharge. To regain the sponge infrastructure in urban and suburban developments, the new approach seeks to integrate retention and infiltration into every lot and curbside. Consequently, new landscape typologies that were previously inconceivable arise and become common terminology.

The greenroof is such an example, now seen more frequently, as many landscapes are actually built on top of structures such as underground garages. The landscape design for the Allianz Arena Munich Stadium is an extensive type of greenroof, which sits on top of a parking garage. The surface is composed of a combination of nonporous and porous asphalt, intended to capture the roof's surface runoff and redirect it to a rain garden for infiltration. While the nonporous asphalt paths facilitate pedestrian movement, the porous asphalt absorbs water and sprout-vegetated islands.

Surface products such as interlocking pavers, concrete, asphalt, as well as structural soils are now designed specifically to manage and attenuate runoff volumes. Various configurations and material compositions allow for a range of retention and infiltration. In the Allianz Arena landscape design, for example, the porous asphalt mix includes lava rock, which increases the surface's water-holding capacity and slows down its release. Structural soils often include super-absorbent polymers (SAP), which absorb up to 400 times their own weight in water in order to increase the soil's water retention and availability for tree roots. Engineered to convey fluids via osmotic pressure, the absorbed water (and fertilizer) is released when the soil is dry. In order to contend with the extreme hydrograph of drought and intermittent torrents, the Besòs River employs a series of inflatable dams along the river that are activated throughout the year. These dams inflate to detain the limited flow and convert the dry riverbed into a continuous cascading pool, and deflate during the onset of a storm to accommodate the torrent.

Set within the context of riverbanks or deltas, water velocity can act as a tremendous erosive force. The Delta In-Channel Island case study employs biotechnical wave and flood control structures in the delta to attenuate erosive coastal wave action, control potential flooding, and improve bank stabilization as well as levee protection.

In Shop Creek, six drop structures were embedded along its course to dissipate the forceful energy of the river during storm events. The structures are wide crescents that turn the flow of the stormwater against itself to decelerate the water's velocity. To prevent erosion of the structures, a mixture of impervious soil cement was applied to form a solidified, protective shell. Other materials discussed within the book, such as geotextiles, bonded fiber matrixes, and cellular soil confinement structures are also frequently applied to prevent erosion, at the same time allowing for vegetation and roots systems to establish and provide stream bank reinforcement.

Weaving Porous and Nonporous Surfaces //
Vogt Landschaftsarchitekten + Herzog & de Meuron

Prior to each game, nearly 70,000 spectators weave through a network of paths that lead up to Allianz Arena soccer stadium. The expanse of pathways accommodates visitors arriving from rail and bus stations, and the parking structure adjoining the arena. The paths meander and climb to the stadium on a greenroof that caps the parking structure.

Designed by Vogt Landscape Architects, the greenroof surface is conceived as a single continuous plane, where combined levels of porosity allow for a hybrid of flows – visitor circulation and stormwater infiltration.

The greenroof surface is constructed of interwoven porous and nonporous substrates, installed flush to form a seamless ground plane. Visually similar, the porous and nonporous areas are distinguished by the respective performance of each substrate. The nonporous asphalt paths accommodate foot and bike traffic, while the porous black lava substrate mimics the black asphalt paths, yet allows for stormwater infiltration, retention, and vegetation growth. THE ARRANGEMENT OF PATHS APPEARS AS IF THEY HAVE BEEN CUT BY ORGANIC FLOWS TRAMPLING PATHWAYS THROUGH A GIANT MEADOW. The porous mix is composed of lava rock, compost, and pumice, with the capacity to retain most of the roof stormwater runoff. Drainage pipes are embedded in the substrate to channel the excess water to the edge of the parking structure, where it is redirected into the surrounding tree-planted soil.

Due to load constraints, the greenroof is extensive (vs. intensive) and therefore the total thickness of the substratum is 20cm (7.8in). The concrete garage roof was waterproofed and applied with a base layer of asphalt, 9–15cm (3.5–5.9in) thick. A top layer consists of 3cm (1.2in) of basalt and chalk stone gravel reinforced asphalt for abrasion resistance.

THE BENEFITS OF THE POROUS AND ABSORPTIVE SURFACE ARE MULTIFOLD. THE INTEGRATED WATER RETENTION SOLUTION MINIMIZED THE NEED FOR A CONVENTIONAL DRAINAGE INFRASTRUCTURE, RESULTING IN COST SAVINGS. ECOLOGICALLY, THE REDUCTION OF PEAK WATER VOLUME DURING RAINSTORM EVENTS PREVENTS POLLUTED RUNOFF FROM ENTERING NEARBY STREAMS AND RIVERS, AND REDUCES FLOODING. Lastly, the reuse of water allows for vegetation growth, which in turn contributes to reducing the heat-island effect, ultimately making the new structure compliant with Germany's permitting process.

1 A weaving of porous and nonporous asphalt surfaces.
2 With the two grades of asphalt the seamless surface allows for vegetation growth.

1

2

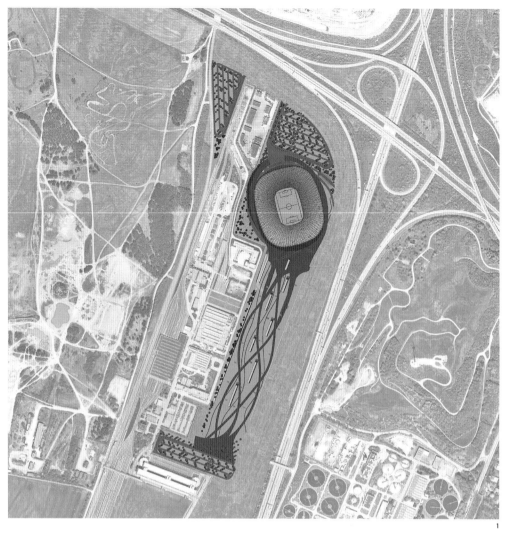

1 The vast expanse of pathways accommodates visitors arriving from nearby rail and bus stations as well as from the parking structure below. 2 The 20cm (8in) substratum and vegetation retain the roof's stormwater runoff. 3 Excessive runoff from the roof surface percolates into the ground. 4 Porous asphalt allows drainage and water retention during rainstorms.

3

4

Inflatable Dam System //

Barcelona Regional Agència Metropolitana de Desenvolupament
Urbanístic i d'Infraestructures S.A.

Environmental Restoration of Besòs River, Barcelona, Spain

The character and composition of the Rio Besòs is in many ways determined by the Mediterranean's rainfall pattern. Rain is scarce for the majority of the year, but during the rainy season torrential rainfall can induce a large surge in the river, turning the dry riverbed into a raging torrent. The force of these intermittent flows is immense and can often devastate the otherwise dormant channel, further eroding its typical barren condition. Naturally, the character of the proposed fluvial park in the Rio Besòs would be determined to a large extent by these extreme conditions.

The Rio Besòs pneumatic dams are a fluvial mechanism agile enough to circumvent some of the constraints of the flood surge. WITH THE FLEXIBILITY OF PNEUMATIC INFRASTRUCTURE EMBEDDED INTO THE LANDSCAPE, THE COMPOSITION OF THE PARK CAN DIRECTLY REACT TO THE VOLATILITY OF THE FLUVIAL SYSTEM. THE RESULT IS A PARK THAT CAN TRANSFORM ITSELF IN A MATTER OF MINUTES TO ACCOMMODATE A SURGE CONDITION.

Eleven dams are distributed through a portion of the Rio Besòs that runs through a densely populated neighborhood. When the river is dormant they create an uninterrupted series of pools, stretching from dam to dam. The pneumatic dams are controlled remotely by a central system and can be adjusted to ensure the right balance between pool areas and water flow, even in drought conditions. Operationally, dams serve to maintain some of the flow characteristics of the river prior to the channel widening. In service of the character of the park, the dams amplify the perceptual impact of the limited water supply. Their placement every 1371ft (400m) creates an illusion of a continuous sheet of water 144ft (44m) wide and more than 2.5mi (4km) long. This adaptable feature is a crucial centerpiece of a fluvial park that is otherwise limited by the river's surge conditions. Because of peak flows river-bottom landscaping is limited to a simple fortified ground of grass and low groundcovers and tall concrete river walls define the park's edges.

The dams are made of inflated rubber cylinders with compressed air, generated from a series of pumping stations embedded in the river channel. The dams inflate in 20min to a height of 4.4ft (1.34m) and a pressure of 2 atmospheres. They can deflate to 80% of their volume in 2min and completely within 15min. THE ANCHORING FOUNDATIONS LIE 5.5IN (14CM) BELOW THE CHANNEL BED, SUCH THAT WHEN THE DAMS DEFLATE, THE ENTIRE MECHANISM IS FLUSH WITH THE RIVERBED, ALLOWING WATER AND DETRITUS TO FLOW DOWNSTREAM UNHINDERED.

During surge conditions the dams deflate in sequence, beginning from the dam furthest downstream, such that the small wave created from the release of the ponds doesn't disturb any dams downstream. With all the dams deflated the park effectively lowers its profile in preparation of the surge event, allowing for maximum flood protection.

1

1

2

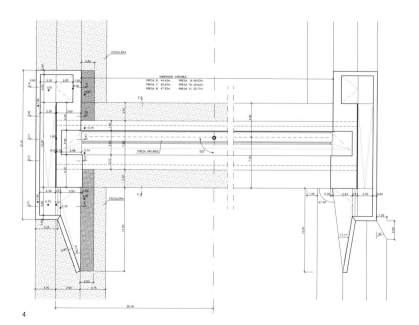

3

1 The dams are inflated to detain water throughout the year and deflate to release the water in a matter of minutes to accommodate a surge condition. **2** Placed every 400m (1,312ft), the dams create an illusion of a continuous river flow 44m (144ft) wide and more than 4km (2.48Ml) long. **3** Eleven dams are distributed through a portion of the Rio Besòs that runs through a densely populated neighborhood. **4** Detail plan of inflatable dam and foundation.

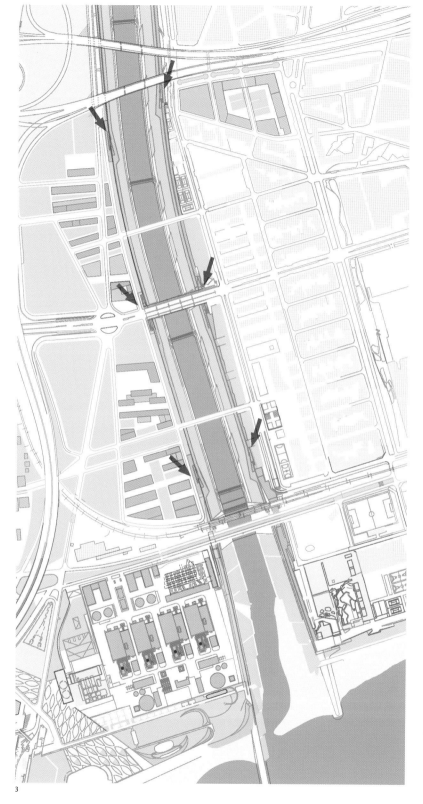

4

Stormwater Garden //
Landworks Studio, Inc.

Blackstone Power Plant Renovation, Harvard University, Cambridge, Massachusetts, USA

As part of Harvard University's ecological initiatives, the Blackstone Power Plant Renovation project is intended to serve as an exemplary prototype for sustainable design solutions. Within this context, landscape architects Landworks Studio, Inc. transformed the 2ac (0.8ha) site into a stormwater garden that would capture and cleanse runoff from an adjacent parking area. Designed to detain a 3-month storm event for 72 hours, the garden captures and cleanses 90% of annual rainfall, consequently preventing polluted runoff and combined sewer overflow from entering nearby rivers and streams.

THE DESIGNERS ENVISIONED THE STORMWATER GARDEN AS A SCULPTURAL EXPRESSION OF WATER MOVEMENT ACROSS THE LANDSCAPE, WHERE "LANDFORMS OF POSITIVE AND NEGATIVE RELIEF" ORCHESTRATE WATER FLOW FROM HIGH POINTS TO LOW POINTS OF COLLECTION AND CONVEYANCE. The garden is composed of two separate courtyards. The Albro Courtyard is a "landform composition of negative relief" where bio-swales function to capture and cleanse runoff from the adjacent parking area. The Blackstone Common Courtyard uses the cut soil from the Albro Courtyard and molds it into a "landform composition of positive relief".

Located along the banks of Charles River, the existing soil on-site was composed of alluvial and marine sediments. Stratified silts, fine sands, with very high clay content (over 65%) rendered the existing soil unsuitable for planting (maximum of 27% clay). Amending the soil or transporting it to a landfill would have been costly. Instead, the proposal included re-using the clay as the structural foundation of the positive landforms in the Common Courtyard, with its interface acting as a drainage conduit to the drainage inlets located in the low points. For the tree planted areas a 6in (15.2cm) layer of coarse sand (S3) was applied over the clay, to remove excess water that will eventually perch above the impervious subgrade; then a 24in (60.7cm) of a support horizon (S2); and lastly a 6in (15.2cm) topsoil layer (S1). For the rest of the planting areas, an 8in (20.3cm) planting soil was applied over the clay subgrade, adequate for the growth of grasses and shrubs.

Carpeted with a seed mix of six Fescue species, named "No Mow Fescue" grass groundcover, only annual mowing is required for the grass to grow to a maximum height of 8–10in (20.3–25.4cm). Bird's Foot Trefoil, Switch Grass, and Tufted Hair Grass complete the ground plane treatment. Wild Raisin Viburnum and Red Osier Dogwood form the understory layer, while Red Maple, River Birch, Honey Locust, and Scarlet Oak accentuate the peaks of the landforms.

The bioretention cell of the Albro Courtyard is a 30 x 100ft (9.1 x 30.5m) linear basin, approximately 3ft (0.9m) below the surrounding grade, which detains 1 to 1¼in (2.5–3.2cm) surface runoff for no longer than 72 hours. A 4ft layer of designed soil positioned above a 1ft (0.3m) layer of sand and below a 3in (7.6cm) layer of organic mulch allows sedimentation, filtration, adsorption, and microbial action to remove pollutants from runoff before it is collected in a crushed-stone and perforated-pipe drainage layer at the bottom of the cell.

A linear crushed-stone diaphragm and a pre-treatment strip decrease the stormwater flow rate, allowing larger particles to settle out before reaching the bottom of the basin. The secondary removal pathways of infiltration and plant resistance and uptake increase the cleansing efficacy of the system.

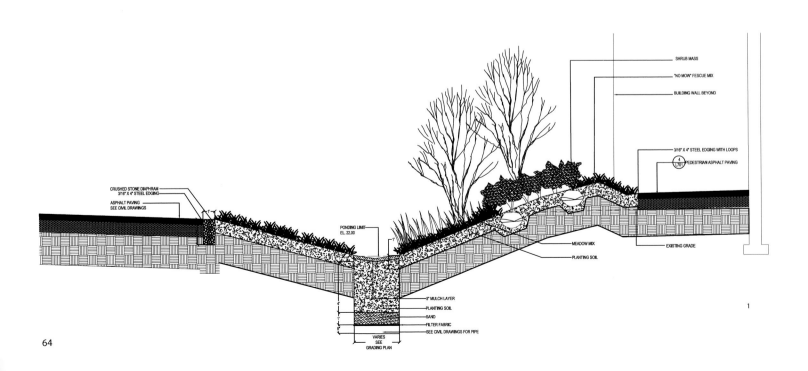

1 A 1ft (0.3m) layer of designed soil was placed over the clay with the clay soil acting as a drainage conduit to the openings in the sides of the drainage inlets located in the low points. **2** Grading plan of landforms and bio-swales.

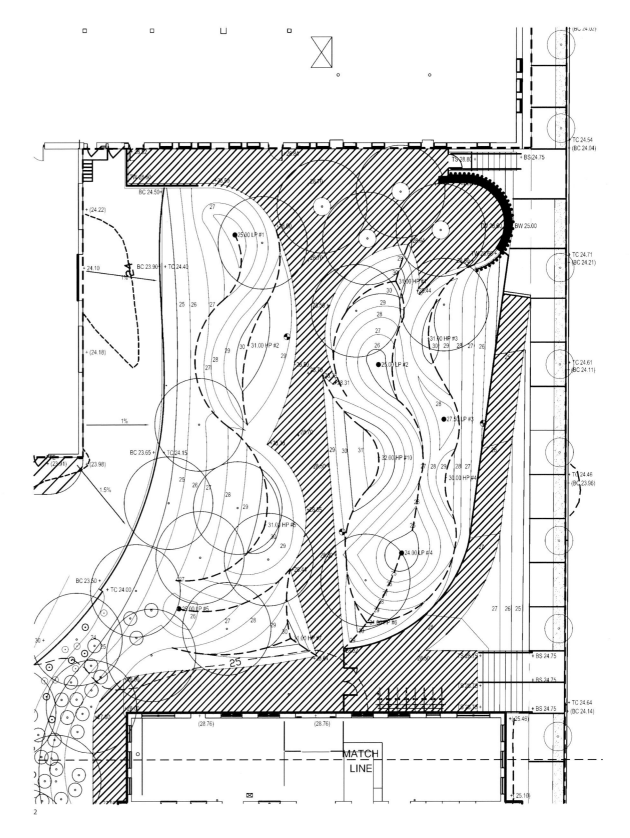

2

1

2

3

1 The clay was designated as the structural foundation of the positive landforms. 2 A seed mix of six Fescue species named "No Mow Fescue" covers the ground plane. 3 The Blackstone Common Courtyard. 4 Illustrated section of designed soil profile and planting strategy. 5 The Albro Courtyard with bio-swale.

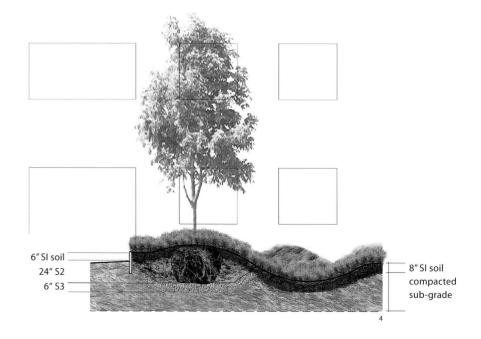

6" Sl soil
24" S2
6" S3

8" Sl soil compacted sub-grade

4

5

Drop Structures for Suburban Stormwater System //
Wenk Associates, Inc. + Mueller Engineering, Inc. + Black & Veatch

Following adjacent suburban developments, Shop Creek became a source of pollution for the Cherry Creek Reservoir, a major recreation area in Aurora, Colorado. Phosphorus, collected by rains from the park and developments, was running into the Creek and feeding algal blooms in the reservoir, killing fish and causing havoc for the ecological and recreational operations of the water body. The banks of Shop Creek itself had been degraded by increased runoff, making it into a lifeless canyon that cuts through a dry plain and provides no ecological or recreational benefits.

The design team for Shop Creek proposed to cut the phosphorus runoff from the creek in half. To do so, the project employs an unusually redundant system that treats the runoff in both a pond and a wetland system.

During storms, the majority of the phosphorus is removed by the upper pond, where the phosphorus and other pollutants settle and are absorbed by sediment. The wetland system, planted with pollutant up-taking cattails and willows, polishes the water released from the pond, augmenting removal of phosphorus and other pollutants. In dry weather conditions, the wetland compensates for the slight release of pollutants from the pond, reducing the outflow's oxygen demand and concentration of organic nitrogen, iron, and suspended solids.

THE WETLAND SYSTEM IS PROTECTED BY SIX DROP STRUCTURES, WHICH ARE EMBEDDED IN THE CREEK AND ACT AS ENERGY DISSIPATERS. THE STRUCTURES ARE WIDE CRESCENTS THAT TURN THE FLOW OF THE STORMWATER AGAINST ITSELF, SLOWING ITS VELOCITY. Additionally, the water is slowed as it interfaces with the increased surface area of the structures' stepped profile. The combination of the pond and drop structures slows the water velocity to 3ft/sec (0.9m/sec) during floods and 0.3ft/sec (0.09m/sec) during small events.

THE MATERIALITY AND INSTALLATION OF THE DROP STRUCTURES INTEGRATE THEM WITHIN THE NATURAL SETTING OF THE PLAIN. SITE SAND AND SOIL WAS MIXED WITH PORTLAND CEMENT AND ROLLED INTO LARGE SOIL-CEMENT CRESCENTS. These were then stacked to shallowly stairstep down the 8ft (2.4m) drops in the streambed. At the bottom of the drop structure a shallow bathtub of soil-cement allows soil buildup and plant growth. A departure from most soil-cement applications, the edges of crescents are left unfinished. The effect is an abstraction of natural outcroppings, further enhanced by incidental erosion of the soil-cement, which slowly marks the patterns of flowing water. Tested to forces up to 400 psi (2.76MPa), the material is able to withstand the force of the creek's flow.

1

2

3

4

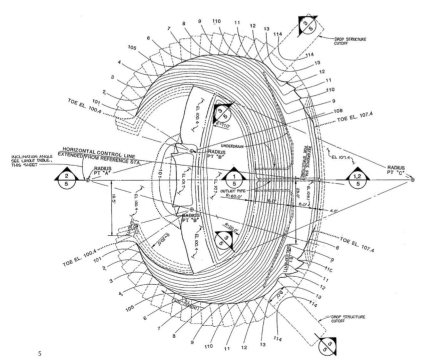

5

6

▓ **1** Six drop structures embedded in the creek. **2** Local sand and soil are mixed with Portland cement, then rolled into the drop structures with a stepped surface to increase surface area. **3** Erosion in the bank before the installation of the drop structures. **4** Drop structures in the wet season. **5** Drop structure section and plan. The drop structures form a wide crescent for energy dissipation. **6** Drop structures in the dry season.

Networked Sidewalk Stormwater System //
Portland Bureau of Environmental Services

SW 12th Avenue Green Street Project, Portland, Oregon, USA

The SW 12th Avenue Green Street project distributes street stormwater treatment between a series of infiltration planters. By distributing the stormwater function, the system can treat a large volume of water within the constraints of an existing street right-of-way. The new street section also accommodates Americans with Disabilities Act (ADA) circulation requirements and substitutes for the typical sidewalk planter strip. The project accomplishes all of this within a linear 8ft(2.4m)-wide strip.

The system of embedded planters is designed to handle 60% of SW 12th Avenue's street runoff, a total of 180,000gl (818.2m³) annually, for the three-lane street with parking. Stormwater runoff from 8000sf (743m²) flows along the existing curb until it reaches the first of four 4ft x17ft (1.2 x 5.2m) stormwater planters, with a combined area of 272sf (25.3m²). A 12in (30.5cm) cut in the curb channels the runoff into the first stormwater planter, which then collects to a level of up to 6in (15.25cm). Once the 6in height is reached, water exits through the planter's second curb cut, along the street, and into the next planter. Only when all the planters exceed capacity will excess water flow into the storm-drain system. It is expected that the water will infiltrate into the ground at a rate of 4in/hr (10.16cm/hr).

During construction, basins were dug to 9in (22.9cm) below the sidewalk grade and filled with native soils, amended with a equal mix of sand, compost, and screened loam. Native Rushes (*Juncus patens*) were planted in rows 18in (45.7cm) on center to allow space for a leaf rake to remove accumulated sediment and debris. During rain events, the native Grooved Rush (*Juncus patens*) in each water

planter slows water-flow and retains pollutants. The rush's deep penetrating roots absorb water and are also drought-tolerant enough to survive the dry summer. Tupelo trees, planted in the middle of each planter, were chosen for their tolerance to wet-dry conditions, and for their spectacular fall color.

The infiltration basins are cleaned of pollutant-loaded sediment periodically. Since installation in July 2005, the first basin in the series has been cleaned every two months, while the others have not yet needed cleaning. Pea gravel placed just below the level of the sediment layers informs excavators when they have reached the bottom of the layer.

Often, the greatest challenge of the design of green streets is accommodating the multiple uses and operations allocated to the parking and sidewalk areas of the street right-of-way. BY DISTRIBUTING HYDROLOGICAL PERFORMANCE THROUGH A NETWORK, THE PROJECT COMPRESSES THE STORM-WATER PLANTERS IN SIZE AND FINDS MORE ROOM FOR PEDESTRI-ANS, ON-STREET PARKING, LANDSCAPING, STREET LIGHTING, AND SIGNAGE.

Since the planters are recessed and not otherwise accessible, a 3ft (0.9m) parking egress zone is required to give people access to their vehicles. Additionally, at each planter a 4in (10.16cm) curb exposure signals the drop in grade, while concrete pavers along the parking egress demarcate a clear separation from the sidewalk zone. ADA accessible grates over the curb cuts allow for unrestricted pedestrian movement in the parking egress zone.

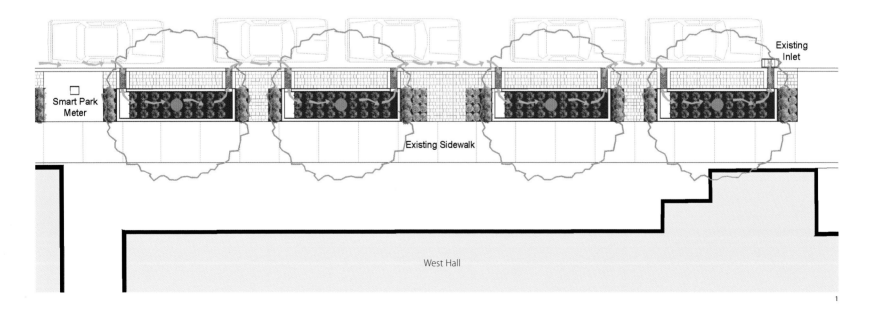

1 Once all planters exceed capacity, excess stormwater flows into the storm-drain system. **2, 3** The 8ft (2.4m) wide street section accommodates stormwater treatment, bike, pedestrian, and ADA accessible circulation. **4** A 12in (30.5cm) cut in the curb channels the street runoff into the first stormwater planter.

2

3

4

Biotechnical Wave & Erosion Control Structures //
MBK Engineers + Kjeldsen Biological Consulting + LSA Associates, Inc.

In light of the hurricane Katrina flood disaster and the 2004 Upper Jones Tract levee failure, which flooded over 10,000ac (4,046ha) of land in the Sacramento-San Joaquin River Delta (SSJRD), California has embarked on an initiative to protect its levees.

The primary focus of this initiative was to stabilize the Sacramento-San Joaquin River Delta In-Channel Islands (ICI) that provide protection for adjacent levees from erosive forces. These islands are remnants of the original Delta Tule marshes, left after dredging or levee construction. Sediment depletion, high channel velocities and wave erosion from watercraft have been destroying the islands, reducing erosion protection, and depleting the tidal refuge these islands provide for estuarine species.

THE DELTA IN-CHANNEL ISLANDS DEMONSTRATION PROJECT TESTED THE EFFECTIVENESS OF USING BIO-TECHNICAL STRUC-TURES AS WAVE AND EROSION CONTROL, AND THE FEASIBILITY OF USING INEXPENSIVE AND RENEWABLE NATURAL-BASED WASTE MATERIALS. 14 different bio-technical wave and erosion control structures were designed, including: log wave-breakers, root wad walls, interlocked root-wads, brush walls, log boom, mulch pillows, ballast buckets, and vegetated stone dikes. Placement of the structures considered location, elevation, substrate nature, and exposure to dynamic forces of daily cycles of tidal flux and seasonal wind fetch. The modular systems were constructed primarily of recycled wood and agricultural fiber waste, such as large woody debris, brush, fibers and roots. Once installed, the structures were vegetated with bulrush called Tule (*Scirpus californicus & Scirpus acutus*). Tule is the dominant inter-tidal vegetation on the marsh islands due to its rapid proliferation and resilience to erosion.

Hydrodynamic monitoring over several years showed that most of the bio-technical structures were highly effective in reducing wave height (by 35% – 64%) and reducing wave energy (by 57% – 87%). Within the parameters of this specific site conditions, brush walls were found to be most effective for reducing wave energy (87%) and for supporting vegetation growth. Log wave-breakers reduced wave energy by 68%; anchored large rootwad by 65%; rootwad wave-breakers by 57%. However, the floating log boom failed within a month of installation.

This project demonstrated the viability of multiple bio-technical methods for decreasing erosive forces and improving bank stabilization as well as levee protection. In some cases, it also showed significant increases in native emergent wetland plant cover and the colonization of aquatic habitat. This experiment can serve as a model for future analysis and design concerning biological erosion control structures, flow hydrodynamic performance, and impact on aquatic and riparian ecologies. Along with their engineering success, these structures have a great potential for formal and aesthetic development.

1

2

3

4

1 Small log wave-breaker. **2** Log wave-breaker. **3** Buttressed log wave-breaker. **4** Floating log boom. **5** Floating log planter/ crib. **6** Peaked stone dike.

5

6

7 Large anchored rootwad. **8** Rootwad wall. **9** Brush wall. **10** Mulch pillow.
11 Drawings in same order as photographs 1–9, and debris pile.

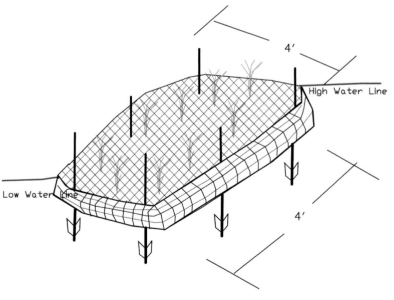

Tethered Floating Log Planter
with Ballast Buckets

Design #2

Tethered Floating Log Planter
with Mulch Pillows

Design #1

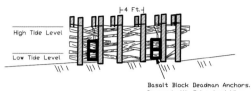

High Tide Level

Low Tide Level

Basalt Block Deadman Anchors.
Secured with Galvanized Wire

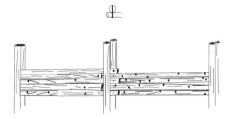

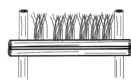

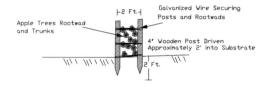

Apple Trees Rootwad
and Trunks

Galvanized Wire Securing
Posts and Rootwads

4' Wooden Post Driven
Approximately 2' into Substrate

2 Ft.

Buttress Support

Untreated Conifer Logs
Pilings Driven into substrate

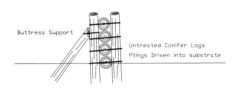

End View
Cross Section

Brush Wall Built to High Water Elevation
Additional Bundles Placed On Top After First Year.
Brush (Fascine) Agricultural Prunings and Recycled Christmas Trees

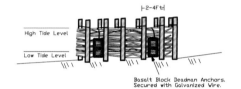

High Tide Level

Low Tide Level

Basalt Block Deadman Anchors.
Secured with Galvanized Wire.

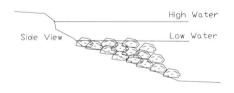

Side View

High Water

Low Water

(Fascine)
Branches Bundled with
Galvanized Wire and
Vineyard Cinches

2 Ft.

2'-4' Fascine

4' Wooden Post Driven
Approximately 2' Into Substrate

2 Ft.

Anchor branches and
Fascine on Soil 4 Ft. On Center

12"X20' Doug Fir
Salt Cured Logs
Secured to Pilings with "U" Bolt

12" Diameter Metal Pipe

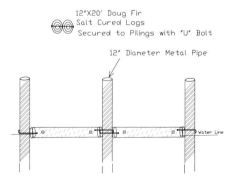

Water Line

Eucalyptus Rootwads Approximatly 36" DBH 8'-10' long

3/4" Galvanized Cables Securing
Rootwad to Deadman Anchor

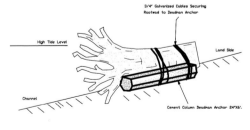

High Tide Level

Land Side

Channel

Cement Column Deadman Anchor 24"X6'.

Rootwads and Anchors Prepared Off-site.
Rootwads and Anchors loaded onto barge and transported to site.
Off-loaded by Crane

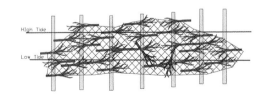

High Tide

Low Tide

11

▦ Grooming

IN THE FOLLOWING PROJECTS, GROOMING TRANSCENDS THE UBIQUITOUS NOTION OF MAINTENANCE AS THE PRESERVATION OF A FIXED STATE, AND INSTEAD ARTICULATES IT AS A RESPONSIVE PATTERN OF CULTIVATION THAT ADVANCES A MORE PHENOMENOLOGICAL READING OF THE LANDSCAPE.

Maintenance is often considered a line of defense within landscape architecture: a set of generic operations that defends a singular design intent from the dynamism of the medium. However, it is this inherent dynamism of the medium, its insistent temporality, that makes the potential relationship of a project and its grooming one of the most interesting and largely overlooked relationships.

In this chapter, Grooming suggests two main objectives. The first is to impart a visible language and experiential form to maintenance operations. The second is to redefine maintenance beyond post-construction management: to broaden its scope to include site preparation, construction process, and post-construction practices as a continuum of actions within an overall design intent.

In the following projects, Grooming transcends the ubiquitous notion of maintenance as the preservation of a fixed state, and instead articulates it as a responsive pattern of cultivation that advances a more phenomenological reading of the landscape. The operations of Grooming dissolve the bias towards a final, designed object, and opt instead for emergence as the design objective.

Grooming recognizes the temporal dynamism of landscape systems and requires that maintenance unfolds as a series of choreographed performances throughout the lifecycle of a landscape site. These operations may be chronologically synchronized, or they may be implemented as parallel and separate systems to be launched simultaneously and combined strategically, but both approaches consider site preparation decisions for ongoing management issues.

Grooming itself is seen here as an abstraction, a life-support technology that corresponds to a set of given or imposed constraints. Within this definition, the materialization of Grooming seeks to blur the concepts of the natural and the artificial. In the Bamboo Garden at Erie Street Plaza, for example, groundwater is converted into steam to create an artificial microclimate in order to sustain a bamboo grove in winter and offer respite for winter joggers.

In the case of the Riem Landscape Park, intensity suppression is exemplified by a strategy of excluding certain vegetal/ecological types, and by rigorous control of quantity and arrangement. Here, Grooming lies primarily within site preparation, controlling the launch of the system during the moment of greatest site manipulation. Paradoxically, the success predicated on the techniques that are used to inhibit dynamism creates a dramatic show of seasonality and mimicry of a pristine system. Anticipating these effects early on in the design process achieves the elimination of excessive post-construction management.

This living system challenges the conventional notions of control versus resilience, of who or what is in control; instead, it posits whether a landscape can be designed to self-propagate, or self-prune. The plasticity of landscape systems is hence defined within the concepts of control of intensity and frequency, as in the function of a sound equalizer. The projects presented are gathered under the guise of adjusting amplification and suppression.

▧ GROOMING RECOGNIZES THE TEMPORAL DYNAMISM OF LANDSCAPE SYSTEMS AND REQUIRES THAT MAINTENANCE UNFOLDS AS A SERIES OF CHOREOGRAPHED PERFORMANCES THROUGHOUT THE LIFECYCLE OF A LANDSCAPE SITE.

Another example of controlled growth is the design for the Elsässertor office building. In order to recreate the contextual railway site within its interior courtyard, and achieve the typical stunted growth pattern of volunteer Beech and Birch trees, 20,000 Beech seedlings were planted in a base of shallow soil and railway gravel. Such an amount of trees would normally suffice for the growth of a two-hectare woodland, yet planted so densely, the trees will attain a purposefully stunted, miniature form.

In the East River Ferry Landings Marsh Planters, plant control of invasive species is integrated into the design. Frequent applications of sprayed saltwater act as an herbicide. The system pumps and disperses surrounding river water, and adjusts to assess the ideal level of frequency and intensity of saltwater application.

Preparation for Grooming can also anticipate and control the quality and physical investment of future maintenance operations. Like a good haircut, a landscape is not merely designed for one defining moment, but is anticipated to grow out in a particular way. The Lurie Garden hedge-trimming armature anticipates the future form of the hedge, synchronizing its growth with its future "haircuts". Freshly planted, the armature acts as the ghost of the future hedge, revealing its intended form before its maturation.

The design for Utrecht University's Library Courtyard Garden employs an apparatus to affect future onsite Grooming as a means to a particular, evolving design vision. In this case, the process of tree-binding creates a "tortured" effect, which points to a

cultural potential that an abstraction, or perversion, of grooming can create; the apparatus emerges as a visual reminder of landscape's pliability.

Grooming suggests an approach in which a site's context and resources, such as wind, bird migration, hydrology, or topography, are reconfigured and harnessed to achieve a controlled and prescriptive emergence. As an example, in Parque de Diagonal Mar, featured in the Launch chapter, the climate-control misting and irrigation system is coordinated with a strategy that utilizes groundwater to prevent the flood-ing of a nearby subway station.

The Products section of the book features several materials that relate to issues of growth control. Rubber mulch is used as a surface treatment, but can also control growth of weeds. Biobarrier® is a subsoil root control geotextile that control-releases a growth-control herbicide. Super-absorbent polymers, also known as Hydrogel, can be used for slow-release irrigation and fertilizer application. The process of Controlled Burning is commonly used in forest management, farming, and prairie restoration to prevent violent fires and to maintain and renew targeted ecosystems by controlling competing vegetation, controlling plant diseases, and perpetuating fire-dependent species.

Adriaan Geuze's basic idea for a garden is a place where life and death come together. In this courtyard garden, death is symbolized by "hell"; the black stones through which red light emanates, and from which "tormented" black mulberry trees grow. Life is represented by the Lilly of the Valley (*Convallaria magalis*) growing in a band around "hell". Distributed throughout the space are red, donut-shaped benches that invite users to stop and become part of the "still life". The enclave is set within Utrecht's University library, serving as a viewing courtyard and a backdrop for the restaurant.

In order to achieve the "fragile, distorted, and twisted, heavy" look of the hell-tortured black mulberry trees, West 8 prescribed a phased-training regiment. The first step called for the trees to be tied to a red powder-coated steel rack in order to begin their sideways growth, as seen in the photographs. Through trial and error, the team found that 4in (10cm) was the largest-diameter tree that could be bent into this shape and then "lean" onto the rack. For this the tree was anchored securely to the ground. Subsequent steps in the process required selective pruning and shape-making until the tree developed into a distinct form and the rack was replaced with a red Dali-esque "crutch" to help carry its advanced weight as well as represent its mortality.

THE SERIES OF CONTROLS APPLIED TO THE TREES CREATE A CEREMONY OF THE OFTEN UNDER-RECOGNIZED TEMPORAL QUALITY OF LANDSCAPE, MAKING VISIBLE THE CHANGE AND MOVEMENT INHERENT IN THE MEDIUM. And although it is the final state of the trees that achieves the full effect of the "torture" qualities, the intermediate red rack is a powerful expression of the process of domination the trees are enduring.

1

1 An illustration of the envisioned "still life". 2 Figuring the largest-diameter tree that could be bent into this shape and then lean onto the "crutch". 3 The tree-binding strategy is a phased-training regimen. 4 The trees are bent and tied to the red "rack".

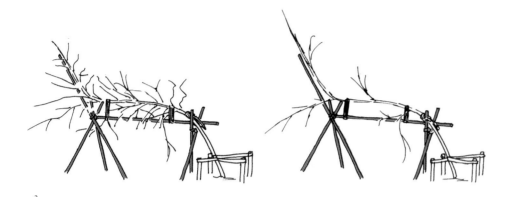

Hedge-Trimming Armature //
Gustafson Guthrie Nichol Ltd. + Piet Oudolf + Robert Israel

The "big shoulders" of the Lurie Garden define the horizon of the garden against the gleaming "headdress" of Gehry's Bandshell to the north, creating an anchor for the intimate garden setting at the center of the park. The Shoulder Hedge protects the interior of the garden from outside elements, notably wind and the heavy pedestrian traffic in Millennium Park. It also defines circulation patterns inside the park, creating a hierarchy of movement between the perennial garden, the hedge, and other elements.

While the shape of the Shoulder Hedge is complex, the system of construction is quite simple, following a few basic design guidelines. The logic of the armature geometry is based on slender steel, 16ft (4.9m) segments. The module allows for the repetition of identical members along the varying curves of the armature and minimizes the need for customized segments. The vertical members along the outer edges of the armature are 14ft (4.3m) tall and tilted slightly inward. Their angle provides for a robust form, giving the giant structure a more intimate scale and allowing for more light to reach the entire surface of the hedge, promoting plant health and full foliage.

EVEN THOUGH THE HEDGE HAS ONLY PARTIALLY FILLED ITS MUSCULAR FORM, THE STEEL ARMATURE ANTICIPATES THE MATURE FORM OF THE TRIMMED VEGETATION. The armature acts as temporary volumetric surrogate and, pragmatically, a profile guide for the future shaping of the plants. Given the scale of the Shoulder Hedge the armature is crucial for unifying the work of the many individuals that will be taking care of the park as well the multiple varieties of plants that grow underneath it.

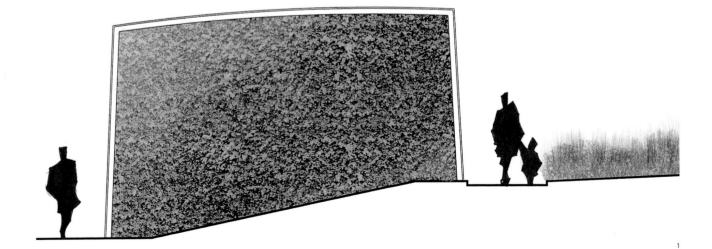

1

1 Illustrated section showing the monumental scale of the hedge. **2** Aerial view of Lurie Garden where the Shoulder Hedge creates a transition between the perennial garden and the bandshell.

2

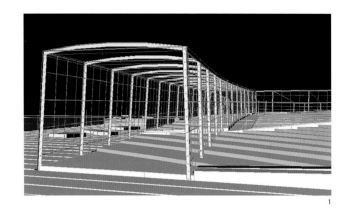

1

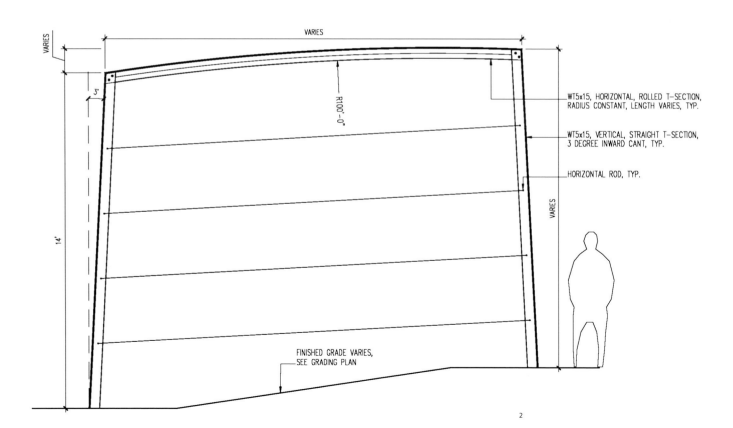

3

VARIES

VARIES

3'

R100'-0"

14'

VARIES

WT5x15, HORIZONTAL, ROLLED T-SECTION,
RADIUS CONSTANT, LENGTH VARIES, TYP.

WT5x15, VERTICAL, STRAIGHT T-SECTION,
3 DEGREE INWARD CANT, TYP.

HORIZONTAL ROD, TYP.

FINISHED GRADE VARIES,
SEE GRADING PLAN

2

1 The armature geometry spans varying lengths of steel segments. 2 The vertical members are tilted slightly inward, which provides a robust form and increased light exposure for the surface. 3 The armature provides a perch for birds. 4 Construction detail of steel frame. 5 The Shoulder Hedge anticipates the mature form of its vegetal interior.

4

5

Artificial Winter Microclimate for a Bamboo Garden //
StoSS Landscape Urbanism

Hybridized Hydrologies, Erie Street Plaza, Milwaukee, Wisconsin, USA

With perhaps the exception of skating rings and sledding hills, urban parks are rarely thought of as a destination during Milwaukee winters. THE DESIGN CONSTRUCTS AN ARTIFICIAL MICROCLIMATE AS A MAINTENANCE STRATEGY TO SUSTAIN VEGETATION IN WINTER AND MAKE THE PARK ACTIVE YEAR-ROUND.

Erie Street Plaza sits at the confluence of Milwaukee's three rivers and the channel to Lake Michigan. "Far beyond the reaches of downtown" this abandoned post-industrial site is what StoSS describes as "a long and cold walk from anywhere". The design advocates the utilization of available on-site water resources to create an unconventional seasonal program.

The park features the Radiant Grove, a series of bamboo planting beds that are integrated with a network of steam pits structured beneath the ground surface. Each steam pit includes a low-energy pump that draws groundwater up from the river below. Immersion heaters in the pits heat up the water to 150°F (65.6°C) and emit hot steam, which creates a warm microclimate within the cold surroundings. This microclimate is intended to sustain the growth of the bamboo during the winter months.

StoSS's illuminated bamboo grove aims to "create a welcome respite from cold winter winds, to warm the hands and bodies of those out for a winter run". The thermal and visual effects at very cold temperatures are envisioned to be impressive, while at warmer temperatures, up to 50°F (10°C), the steam effect is "visible but more ethereal". Visitors are envisioned to stroll through the "otherworldliness of this artificial ecology". As winter fades and spring temperatures rise above 50°F (10°C) the system shuts off until next winter.

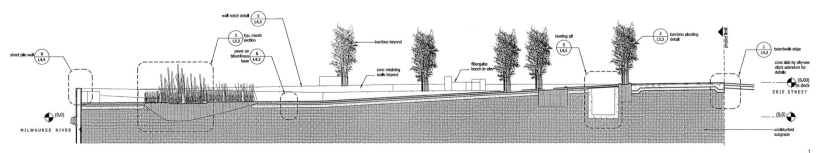

1 The bamboo planting beds are integrated with subground steam pits that draw water from the river. 2 Constructing an artificial microclimate in order to make the park active year-round.

2

1 Detail of steam pit. **2** The radiant grove provides a warm destination in winter. **3** As winter fades and spring temperatures rise above 50°F (10°C) the system shuts off.

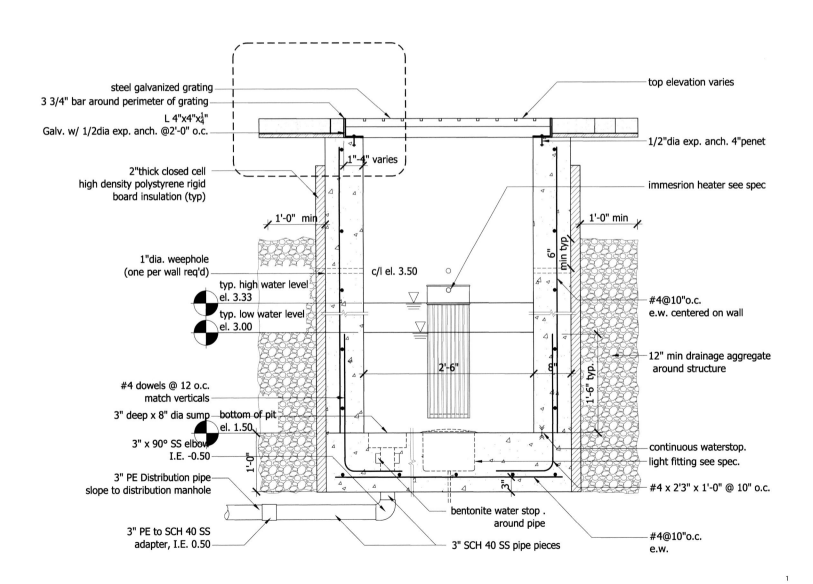

steel galvanized grating

3 3/4" bar around perimeter of grating

L 4"x4"x$\frac{1}{4}$"
Galv. w/ 1/2dia exp. anch. @2'-0" o.c.

2"thick closed cell
high density polystyrene rigid
board insulation (typ)

1'-0" min

1"dia. weephole
(one per wall req'd)

typ. high water level
el. 3.33

typ. low water level
el. 3.00

#4 dowels @ 12 o.c.
match verticals

3" deep x 8" dia sump

3" x 90° SS elbow
I.E. -0.50

3" PE Distribution pipe
slope to distribution manhole

3" PE to SCH 40 SS
adapter, I.E. 0.50

1'-4" varies

c/l el. 3.50

2'-6"

bottom of pit
el. 1.50

1'-0"

bentonite water stop .
around pipe

3" SCH 40 SS pipe pieces

top elevation varies

1/2"dia exp. anch. 4"penet

immesrion heater see spec

1'-0" min

6" min typ

8"

1'-6" typ.

3"

#4@10"o.c.
e.w. centered on wall

12" min drainage aggregate
around structure

continuous waterstop.
light fitting see spec.

#4 x 2'3" x 1'-0" @ 10" o.c.

#4@10"o.c.
e.w.

1

2

3

Saltwater Herbicide System //
Ken Smith Landscape Architect

Pounded by severe wakes from ocean-going boats, the vertical concrete banks of the East River defy traditional riparian restoration tactics. The Marsh Planters do not propose a "restoration", but present a different strategy, one that balances restoration intentions with the present set of urban forces.

THE PLANTERS ARE CONCEIVED AS A RIPARIAN MODULE, AN ECOLOGICAL ABSTRACTION OF THE RANGE OF PLANTS THAT OCCUPY THE RIPARIAN ZONE. EACH PLANTER MODULE IS FOLDED TO SIMULATE THE SLOPE OF A NATURAL RIVERBANK, WITH THE INTENTION OF RECREATING THE PHYSICAL AND HYDROLOGICAL CONDITIONS OF LOW MARSH AND HIGH MARSH. The planters are suspended off a 90ft (27.4m) long pier on a typical I-beam pier structure in order to protect the vegetation from the harsh wakes.

Saltwater grasses (*Spartina alterniflora*) are planted in the eight 10ft x 15ft (3.0m x 4.6m) steel planter boxes. They are planted in a substrate consisting of sand mixed with an organic compost mix and a water-retaining layer of Hydrogel – a super-absorbent polymer, capable of retaining 200 to 400 times its own weight in water. This acts as a replacement for the underlying mud layer found in natural marsh conditions, which prevents the roots from drying out from wind exposure. Despite their common sighting in brackish or saltwater conditions, Ken Smith's

team found that *Spartina*, cultivated in nurseries, actually grows more successfully in containers submerged in, or irrigated with freshwater. However, brackish water works well as an herbicide, deterring weedy plant species un-adapted to salt-water. THUS THE PLANTERS UNDERGO TWO IRRIGATION REGIMES: FRESHWATER FOR DAILY IRRIGATION AND BRACKISH WATER ON A WEEKLY CYCLE. THE BRACKISH EAST RIVER WATER IS PUMPED UP AND SENT THROUGH EXPOSED CHANNELS TO FLOOD THE BOXES AND ACT AS AN HERBICIDE.

In addition to working as an herbicide the periodic pumping of brackish water into the constructed marsh also introduces nutrients, minerals, and larvae (invertebrate macrofauna) including fiddler crab, ribbed mussels, and salt marsh snails. This interaction, along with the porous bottom of the steel planters, allows for "a modified land-water interaction" similar to a natural marsh condition.

For Ken Smith, the main objective of this design is to allow the irrigation system to be "flexible for both experimental and maintenance issues". Depending on initial results, East River water could be used exclusively to irrigate the plants, or could be mixed at different concentrations with freshwater. Individual boxes are also controllable, resulting in a simple and easily manipulated system where "small-scale urban experiments" can occur.

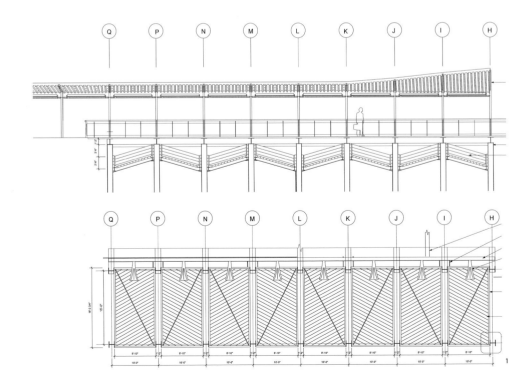

1 Saltwater grasses (*Spartina alterniflora*) are planted in the eight 10ft x 15ft (3m x 4.6m) steel planter boxes. **2** Brackish water is pumped to flood the boxes and act as an herbicide, deterring invading weedy plant species.

MHHW Mean High High Water: The highest tide recorded.
MHW Mean High Water: Average high tide.
MHD Manhattan Highway Datum, point set by the Department of Transportation.
MLW Mean Lower Water.

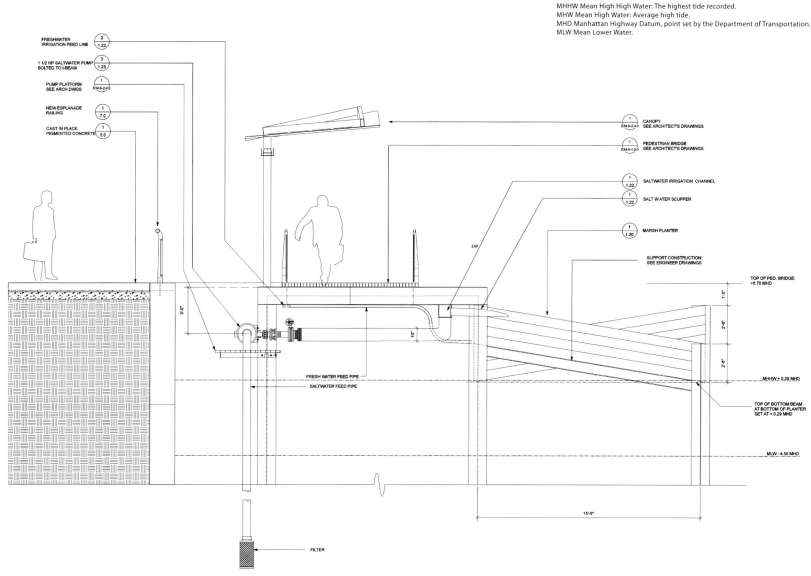

FRESHWATER
IRRIGATION FEED LINE

1 1/2 HP SALTWATER PUMP
BOLTED TO I-BEAM

PUMP PLATFORM
SEE ARCH DWGS

NEW ESPLANADE
RAILING

CAST IN PLACE
PIGMENTED CONCRETE

CANOPY
SEE ARCHITECT'S DRAWINGS

PEDESTRIAN BRIDGE
SEE ARCHITECT'S DRAWINGS

SALTWATER IRRIGATION CHANNEL

SALT WATER SCUPPER

MARSH PLANTER

SUPPORT CONSTRUCTION:
SEE ENGINEER DRAWINGS

TOP OF PED. BRIDGE:
+6.70 MHD

FRESH WATER FEED PIPE

SALTWATER FEED PIPE

MHHW + 0.39 MHD

TOP OF BOTTOM BEAM
AT BOTTOM OF PLANTER
SET AT + 0.29 MHD

MLW - 4.50 MHD

FILTER

15'-0"

2

1 The planters are suspended off a 90ft (27.6m) long pier on a typical I-beam pier structure in order to protect the vegetation from the harsh wakes. **2** Each riparian module is folded to simulate the slope of a natural riverbank.

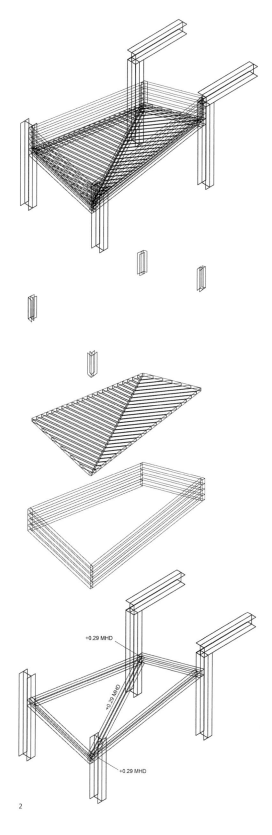

+0.29 MHD

+0.29 MHD

+0.29 MHD

1

2

Remarkably few, if any, weeds established themselves during the large-scale perennial installation of Heiner Luz's Iris-Mint meadow and Cane-Brake slope at the Riem Landscape Park in Munich. The maintenance regime prescribed weeding during establishment, but the planting is otherwise designed to require little subsequent spot maintenance. CONTROLLING MEADOW PLANTINGS TO EXPRESS FORMAL DESIGN INTENTIONS REQUIRES A STRATEGY THAT BOTH MINIMIZES MAINTENANCE AND IMPROVES THE INTEGRITY OF THE PLANTING, GIVEN THE NATURALLY SUCCESSIONAL TENDENCIES OF MEADOWS, THE THOUSANDS OF INDIVIDUAL PLANTS, AND THE UBIQUITOUS PRESENCE OF INVASIVE PLANTS.

For Heiner Luz, the "principle of leading aspect" provides the foundation for successful design with meadow plantings. The principle merges his design rule of "uniformity on a large scale and variety on a small scale" with his own insights into natural conditions, in particular the observation that a few species dominate in every plant grouping. In general, the principle dictates a dominant species in the meadow mix that creates the "leading aspect" of the vegetation image. Dominant establishment and self-propagation of these species maintain a design vision over time. In general the "leading aspect" occurs 2 – 4 times per m^2 while companions occur at most once per m^2 or even only once every 2 to 4m^2. In the Iris-Mint meadow and the Cane-Brake slope-shrub meadows, Iris-Mint and Cane-Brake are the "leading aspects".

Following this principle, Heiner Luz planted the "shrub meadows" with 10 – 12 shrubs / m^2 (8 – 10 shrubs / y^2) to mimic the 25 – 30 / m^2 (20 – 24 / y^2) individuals found in typical meadow societies and in order to form a ground vegetation as quickly as possible to stop the growth of weeds.

The second important aspect of the planting strategy was the mulch layer. The perennial plantings at the lake slopes were mulched with a bright gray granite gravel in a thickness of 5cm (2in) on average. The mulch layer was applied prior to the planting procedure and was selectively removed during the planting. Mineral mulch has a number of advantages over typical mulches, beyond its superior effectiveness in preventing weed growth. With mineral mulch the capillaries of the soil are interrupted, so that less humidity evaporates and water availability for the plants improves. It is an improvement over bark mulch in that it does not extract nutrients from the soil and the dry surface is not vulnerable to fungi infestation.

Together the "principle of leading aspect" and the application of the mineral mulch have overcome the maintenance issue endemic with planted meadows and enabled it to become a viable design form within reach of civic parks and landscapes. The effect of the planting is a spectacular seasonal show, exhibiting a dynamic character rarely sustainable at such a large temporal and spatial scale.

1

2

1 Distribution of topsoil. **2** The plantings were mulched 5cm (2in) thick with a gray granite gravel. **3** The meadow during summer bloom.

3

1 The shrub meadows were planted with 10–12 shrubs/m² (8–10 shrubs/y²)to mimic the 25–30/m² (20–24/y²) found in typical meadow. 2 Park path following planting. 3 The meadow during fall bloom.

3

Stunted Growth Pattern //
Vogt Landschaftsarchitekten + Herzog & de Meuron

Elsässertor office building, Basel, Switzerland

The Elsässertor office building is located on the site of a decommissioned railroad track. Designed by Vogt Landscape Architects in collaboration with the architectural design of Herzog & de Meuron, the landscape design references the site's railroad vernacular and derelict landscape typology. It adopts the unusual nature of railroad tracks, where volunteer ecologies persistently grow from the gravel bed and thrive within the harsh growing conditions.

Vogt's planting selection draws upon the typical degraded soil conditions in the regional context of Jura, Switzerland, where Beech, Birch and Locust trees are often found as volunteer species. Volunteer or pioneer species are the first species to colonize or re-colonize a barren or disturbed area due to their tremendous resilience and adaptability. Yet, despite their ability to establish in soil-less, nutrient-poor aggregate such as railway gravel ballast, their formation often results in a stunted growth pattern. For the landscape of the Elsässertor project, Vogt extracted these attributes and reconstructed them within the context of the building. INSIDE THE OFFICE BUILDING, TWO LIGHT-WELL COURTYARDS, WHICH PROJECT UP FROM THE SECOND LEVEL TO THE ROOF, CONTAIN SIX FRAMED PLANTING BEDS, PLANTED WITH 20,000 COMMON BEECH TREE BARE-ROOT SEEDLINGS, AN AMOUNT WHICH WOULD NORMALLY SUFFICE FOR THE GROWTH OF A TWO-HECTARE WOODLAND. The substrate for the planting consists of a non-organic lava-pumice mineral mixture, embedded with drip irrigation, and topped by railway gravel ballast. Planted in such high density and into a very shallow soil substratum, the beech trees were envisioned as a grove of miniature trees.

The planting beds are integrated and orientated at an angle according to the building's interior glass ceiling structure that provide light for the floor below. The structure features a three-dimensional geometry of intersecting metal beams, framing a triangular geometry of glass and planting beds. This geometry invokes the image of railroad steel tracks, crossing and splitting into diverging routes, as the railway ecology emerges within the building through the recreation of the stunted growth pattern of the unrelenting railway vegetation.

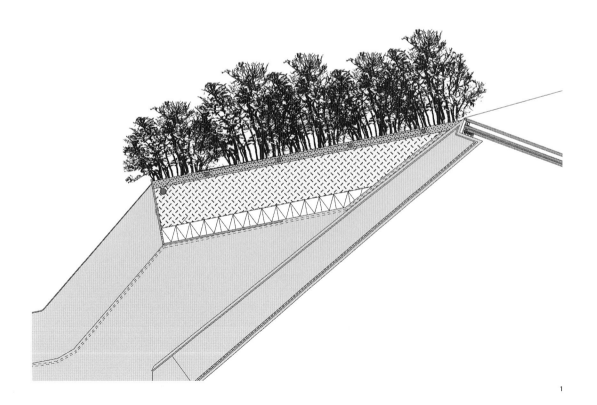

1

2

1 Planting 20,000 Beech tree bare-root seedlings – an amount sufficient for a 2ha woodland. 2 Two light-well courtyards contain six framed planting beds.

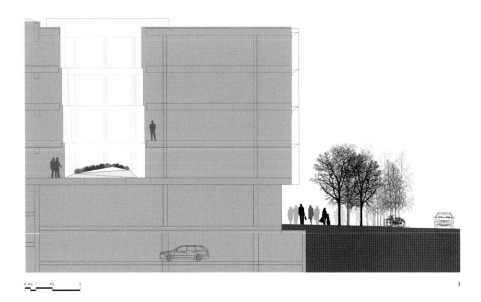

1 Section-elevation. 2 Plan of three courtyards, two of which feature the railroad ecology planters. 3 Construction of the planter, sealed with a geomembrane liner. 4 Substrate consists of lava-pumice mineral mixture with drip irrigation. 5 The top layer consists of railway gravel.

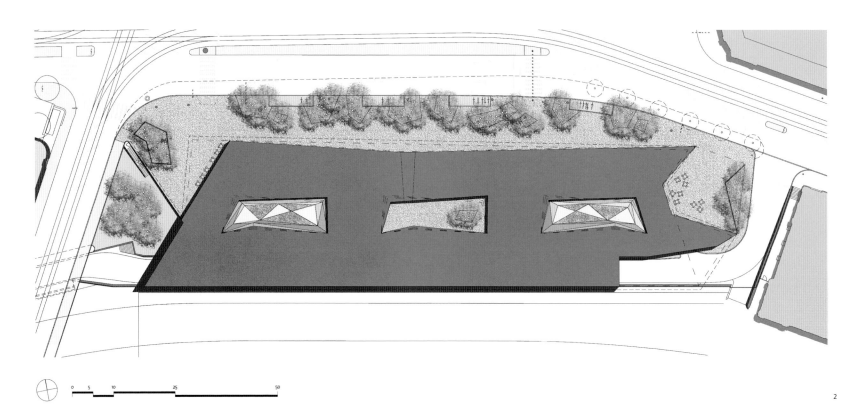

3

4

5

Digestive

THE DIGESTIVE CHAPTER EXAMINES THE METABOLIC OPERATIONS OF MATERIAL RESOURCES, WHETHER LIVING OR NONLIVING. HERE, METABOLISM PERTAINS TO PHYSICAL AND CHEMICAL PROCESSES, BY WHICH MATERIAL RESOURCES ARE GENERATED, RETAINED, BALANCED, RECONFIGURED, OR BIODEGRADED INTO NEW RESOURCES.

Topics of site-remediation techniques for the treatment and reclamation of post-industrial residue or disturbed ecologies have been widely discussed in the last decade within the field of landscape architecture. Bio-remediation and phytore-mediation techniques highlight the capacity of plants and associated bacteria to absorb or process harmful chemicals and excess nutrients, granting landscape architecture expanded performance criteria that were previously considered solely within the field of ecology and engineering.

The Digestive chapter examines the metabolic operations of material resources, whether living or nonliving. Here, metabolism pertains to physical and chemical processes, by which material resources are generated, retained, balanced, reconfigured, or biodegraded into new resources. All materials and processes are considered in terms of input and output within a food chain, whether nutritious, innocuous, excessive, or harmful. Within this context, material resources are always in a state of flux. For example, pollutants or excess nutrients are conveyed via air and water flow across site boundaries. Since many contemporary sites are inherited with a history of preceding uses, existing materials such as stone or concrete are often designated for removal offsite. Digestive operations consider migrations of resources as opportunities and constraints for design principles.

Until recently, pollutants or excess materials have been transported offsite to centralized systems for storage (landfill) or processing (sewage treatment plants). With rising energy costs and stricter dumping or discharging protocols, this paradigm has begun to shift to in-situ strategies. In addition, reliance on decentralized and bio-based processes that intend to meet or exceed physical and economic performance has been rapidly increasing, and has been followed by new opportunities for site-specific integration of a spatial, aesthetic, and experiential form.

Sidwell Friends School features a closed-loop system of water recycling, which processes the school's wastewater in a series of outdoor wetland gardens to be reused within the building. Both the SW 12th Avenue Green Street Project and the Blackstone Stormwater Garden featured in the Fluid chapter incorporate a decentralized bio-based system for integrated stormwater treatment. Designed with a capacity to retain rainfall during storm events, networked planters and bio-swales intercept polluted sediment migration before the sediment reaches nearby water bodies.

Digestive classifies operations in terms of two distinct but congruent scales: micro and macro. Micro encompasses plant, bacterial, or fungal nutrient conversion or uptake; macro defines the larger scale of earthworks, cut and fill, and concealment. Digestive further categorizes such operations according to two distinct time sequences: a one-time operation and an ongoing, managed operation. These scales relate to the sources and locations of materials in a variety of ways.

Water-based resources, such as stormwater surface runoff or building wastewater, are typically categorized within a continual time sequence that requires micro-digestion. For example, the Water-Cleansing Biotope at the DaimlerChrysler Potsdamer Platz plaza continually metabolizes excess nutrients in rainwater collected from 13

UNTIL RECENTLY, POLLUTANTS OR EXCESS MATERIALS HAVE BEEN TRANSPORTED OFFSITE TO CENTRALIZED SYSTEMS FOR STORAGE (LANDFILL), OR PROCESSING (SEWAGE TREATMENT PLANTS). WITH RISING ENERGY COSTS AND STRICTER DUMPING OR DISCHARGING PROTOCOLS, THIS PARADIGM HAS BEGUN TO SHIFT TO IN-SITU STRATEGIES.

surrounding buildings through a combination of filter substrate and water plants. Various substrates and materials are currently being studied for their capacity to biodegrade excess nutrients or harmful compounds in wetlands, biotopes, and bio-swales.

The restoration of the Besòs River addresses a different site context and digestive configuration. Subsurface wetlands are embedded in a riverbed to intercept and treat sewage effluent below the ground surface using plants and bacteria to take up excess nutrients or biodegrade chemicals. The digested water then becomes the river's source of flow during dry weather. In contrast, the BioHaven™ Floating Islands introduce a mobile Digestive system deployed within water bodies. As with stationary wetland structures, mobile islands foster the natural uptake of pollutants and establish their own habitat and food chain.

Airborne chemicals also require methods to intercept and biodegrade the migration of pollutants. Photocatalytic cement traps and then decomposes airborne pollutants into innocuous elements; Naturaire® vertical plantscape is designed to take up or break down interior airborne pollutants.

Soil-based resources may combine the two scales of Digestive operations by employing both biological remediation via plants, bacteria, or fungus (mycoremediation), as well as macro strategies of cut and fill or concealment (capping). For example, the former British Petroleum Park combines three different Digestive operations: onsite soil bio-remediation; the introduction of coastal wetlands to con-tinually cleanse polluted runoff; and the reuse of the site's infrastructure in order to redirect runoff to the wetlands.

Cultuurpark Westergasfabriek and the Urban Outfitters Navy Yard best exemplify macro-Digestive strategies, reconfiguring site materials to contribute to determining circulation, topography, plantings, and program. The former sets up strategies of polluted soil cut and fill, while the latter reuses the existing inorganic concrete surface to create a porous and vegetated surface.

Bio-Remediation Park Design //
McGregor+Partners

Former British Petroleum Park, Sydney, Australia

Located on the Waverton Peninsula in North Sydney, the 2.5ha (6.2ac) former British Petroleum Park exemplifies the use of on-site processes to clean and maintain an industrially contaminated site. On-site processes include both soil cleansing and the repurposing of industrial infrastructure for ongoing site operations.

As a British Petroleum (BP) storage depot the site held 31 oil tanks and ancillary facilities that stood on massive concrete platforms sitting in spaces carved from the sandstone bedrock. While the tanks and structures were eventually removed, a legacy of soil contamination and site infrastructure remained.

Prior to construction of the park, BP Australia was required to clean the contaminated soil. RATHER THAN EXCAVATING AND PLACING THE CONTAMINATED SOIL IN A LANDFILL, THEY EMPLOYED ON-SITE BIO-REMEDIATION TECHNIQUES TO DECONTAMINATE THE TOPSOIL. Topsoil was stripped, stockpiled on site, and mixed with organic compost and Effective Microorganisms (EM), a liquid soil-enhancer product from Japan. The stockpiled soil was turned every three months, and after nine months of repeated testing, the soil was re-used across the site as a planting medium.

Following soil preparation, McGregor+Partners coordinated the planting of approximately 95,000 seedlings to restore the natural coastal sandstone woodlands. Native seed stock was collected from nearby bushland reserves, propagated, and used as plant stock.

McGregor+Partners' design for the park repurposes the site's industrial fragments as both a means to create natural landscape conditions and to contain any remaining contamination. The site's abandoned stormwater infrastructure was retrofitted to redirect stormwater into frog habitat ponds, located at the base of sandstone cliffs. The ponds detain and treat the site's stormwater and prevent any remaining traces of on-site contamination from entering Sydney Harbor. They also anchor the site's design and become a central area of focus.

STEEL PLATFORMS DELICATELY WEAVE THROUGH AND PROJECT ABOVE THE PRESERVED SANDSTONE CLIFFS, ALLOWING FOR VIEWING OF THIS EMERGING LANDSCAPE. The newly established framework and ongoing decontamination processes provide new habitat, as well as an impressive shoreline feature.

1

2

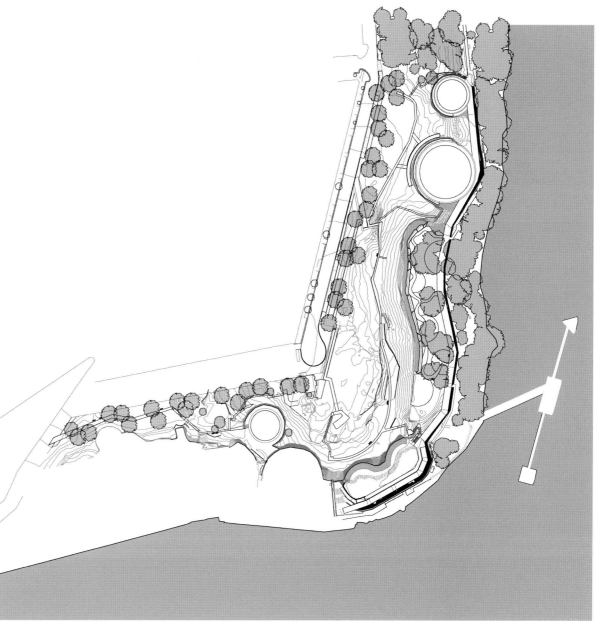

1 Wetlands encircle the former BP drum location. 2 Aerial photos of existing conditions after removal of drums and of constructed park. 3 Plan showing the concrete platforms, where the drums once stood, as they relate to the stormwater detention wetlands.

3

1 Stormwater detention wetlands are designed to intercept any remaining contamination prior to entering Sydney Harbor. **2** Steel grating hovers above the preserved sandstone cliffs. **3** Biofiltration ponds and water control pit. **4** The emergent landscape and Sydney's skyline.

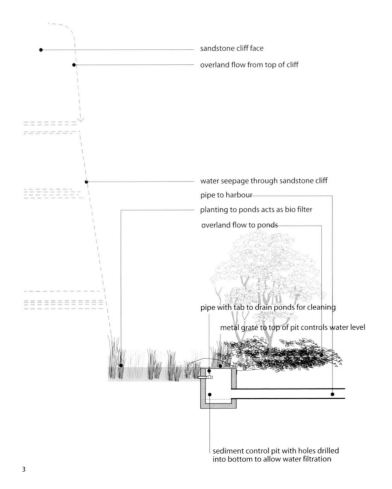

sandstone cliff face

overland flow from top of cliff

water seepage through sandstone cliff

pipe to harbour

planting to ponds acts as bio filter

overland flow to ponds

pipe with tab to drain ponds for cleaning

metal grate to top of pit controls water level

sediment control pit with holes drilled
into bottom to allow water filtration

3

4

Fluvially Integrated Effluent Wetlands //
Barcelona Regional, Agència Metropolitana de Desenvolupament Urbanístic i d'Infraestructures S.A.

Environmental Restoration of Besòs River, Barcelona, Spain

In 1996, when the European Union commissioned the restoration of the Rio Besòs, the river was considered one of the most polluted in Europe. The Besòs, one of two rivers which bound the Barcelona metropolitan area and serve a large, heavily urbanized basin, suffered from a variety of malaises, both from environmental stresses and engineering. High demand for water had depleted the river's flow to the point that in dry seasons the flow regime of the river was largely determined by effluent discharges from wastewater treatment plants. The river was also subject to a torrential rainfall pattern, which after the basin's development often led to floods, some dangerous enough that the river was channelized. In the rainy season the river can swiftly transform from a dry riverbed into a raging torrent, threatening adjacent property and inhabitants and dislodging established riverbed ecologies.

In order to improve the quality of the dry season river water sources, 60 water treatment wetlands were embedded within the channel in the upper, less developed reaches. These sub-surface treatment wetlands serve as tertiary treatment areas for the direct flows from adjacent wastewater treatment plants. Sub-surface wetlands are better adapted to the flow patterns of the river, minimize evaporation, unseemly smells and mosquitoes, while increasing the surface area for effluent treatment. The beds themselves vary in length and width, averaging 50m (164ft) in width and 20m (65.6ft) in length, with flow rates between 0.3 – 0.4m3/sec (10.6 – 14.1cf/sec). The polished water exits from the wetlands via a drainage system that ensures that all of the water is treated. Excess biomass is periodically removed from the beds and used as a substrate. Effluent from the beds is used to water vegetation on the riverbanks.

By embedding this extensive wetlands system into a fluvial channel, Barcelona Regional has increased the utility and quality of the entire river system. THE WETLANDS SERVE MULTIPLE FUNCTIONS LOCALLY, PROVIDING HABITAT, VISUAL INTEREST, AND IRRIGATION. THEY ALSO SERVE THE RIVER SYSTEM AS A WHOLE BY POLISHING ITS PRIMARY DRY SEASON WATER SOURCE. THE WETLANDS DEMONSTRATE THE POTENTIAL OF LAYERING MULTIPLE USES WITHIN INFRASTRUCTURAL LANDSCAPE TO SERVE THE GOALS OF INCREASED ECOLOGICAL INTEGRITY AND HUMAN AMENITY.

1

1 Section of tertiary treatment wetlands in flood plane and in relation to the canal. **2** The wetlands capture and treat effluent released from adjacent sewage treatment plants. **3** 60 water treatment wetlands were embedded within the channel in the upper, less-developed reaches serving as tertiary treatment areas for the direct flows originating from the adjacent wasterwater treatment plants.

2

3

3

1 Construction of the wetland within the riverbed. 2 The beds vary in length and width, averaging 50m (164ft) wide and 20m (65.6ft) long, with flow rates between 0.3–0.4m³/sec (10.6–14.1cf/sec). 3 Planting the subsurface wetlands. 4 Tertiary wetland treatment for dry-season water source.

4

Water-Cleansing Biotope //
Atelier Dreiseitl

Stormwater runoff from rooftops is relatively uncontaminated and has low nutrient concentrations. Yet, despite low concentrations, the cumulative impact on natural waterways is detrimental and necessitates decontamination of even trace pollutants. This need, combined with stringent water conservation policies, becomes a platform for inventive strategies for the cleansing and reuse of stormwater.

Atelier Dreiseitl treats these hydrological considerations as central elements in their innovative design for Berlin's Potsdamer Platz. Constructed on top of a traffic tunnel that connects Berlin's Tiergarten park and the Spree to the north of the city, the design orchestrates collection, reuse and filtration processes for stormwater runoff collected from surrounding rooftops. Once collected, the stormwater is circulated within a publicly interactive open-air water feature. There, a series of cleansing biotopes filter the water before it overflows into the nearby river. THE CLEANSING BIOTOPES ARE A FORM OF CONSTRUCTED WETLANDS THAT ARE PARTICULARLY EFFECTIVE FOR STORMWATER TREATMENT. THIS EFFECTIVENESS STEMS FROM THEIR FAST WATER CIRCULATION AND HIGHLY EFFICIENT METABOLISM OF EXCESS NUTRIENTS. What sets them apart from conventional stormwater filtration systems is that they are chemical-free.

Fast circulation is critical in order to reduce algae growth. An influx of high pollutant concentrations can stimulate excessive algae growth. This enhanced plant growth, often called an algal bloom, reduces dissolved oxygen in the water, thus causing nutrient-digesting microorganisms to die and disrupting the normal functioning of the ecosystem. Fast water circulation ensures sufficient oxygen loads and allows for a balanced uptake of nutrients by plants and related microorganisms.

With a cistern volume of 35,315cf (1,000m³), the entire collected stormwater is circulated through the sequence of biotopes within three days in order to reduce algae growth. The biotope's substrate depth and composition facilitate this fast circulation with a relatively shallow, non-organic, low-nutrient sand-mineral mix that is highly porous. The three-layer filter substrate is composed of 90% sand, 5% mineral additives (zeolite), and 5% lava rock. The zeolite mineral has a high permeabil-

ity coefficient and a high nutrient-fixing capacity. The red lava rock with an iron content of up to 15% can significantly increase the phosphate-binding capability. Round sand particles, 1–3mm (1/100–1/10in) in size, ensure a specific void ratio and hence porosity in the substrate, critical to plant growth.

As the plants are normally accustomed to growing in an organic substrate, an entire growing period was dedicated to adaptation in a non-organic growing medium off-site, before planting them in the biotope. Additionally, since the biotopes have low nutrient loads, potted plants were densely spaced in order to overcome the initial malnourishment and compensate for any related loss of plant material. Planting at the edges of the cleansing biotope assist in the uptake of nutrients and oxygenation of the water. The year-round input of oxygen into the system prevents the re-release of phosphates and therefore an effective binding capacity is set in place for many years.

Cleansing biotopes are very efficient in decomposing both particulate and dissolved organic materials. Oxygen-fed aquatic microorganisms that live in symbiosis with plant roots facilitate the decomposition of organic carbon composites. With the vast surface of the substrate matrix and of plants roots, these microfauna can spread widely. Oxygen load is provided by water input, while plants contribute additional oxygen as well as carbon dioxide through their root system. Bacteria then nitrify ammonium in the presence of oxygen, while the plants partially feed off the nitrates. This digestive system has demonstrated continual endurance. The Potsdamer Platz biotopes have been operational for over eight years. ASIDE FROM MAINTAINING A CHEMICAL BALANCE OF DISSOLVED LIME AND MOWING THE PLANTS ONCE A YEAR, THE SYSTEM AND SUBSTRATE REQUIRE VERY LITTLE MAINTENANCE. UNLIKE TRADITIONAL SAND FILTER SYSTEMS, REPLACING THE SUBSTRATE OR REMOVING THE UPPER LAYERS IS GENERALLY NOT NECESSARY. Only under extreme conditions, where the substrate becomes clogged and the circulation volume drops dramatically, would the cleansing biotope have to be emptied and re-established.

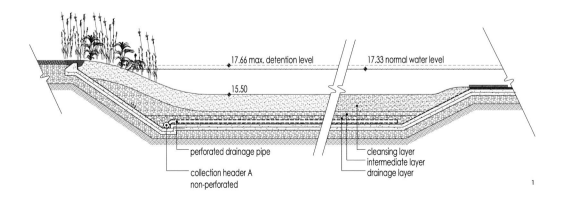

17.66 max. detention level   17.33 normal water level

15.50

perforated drainage pipe

collection header A
non-perforated

cleansing layer
intermediate layer
drainage layer

1

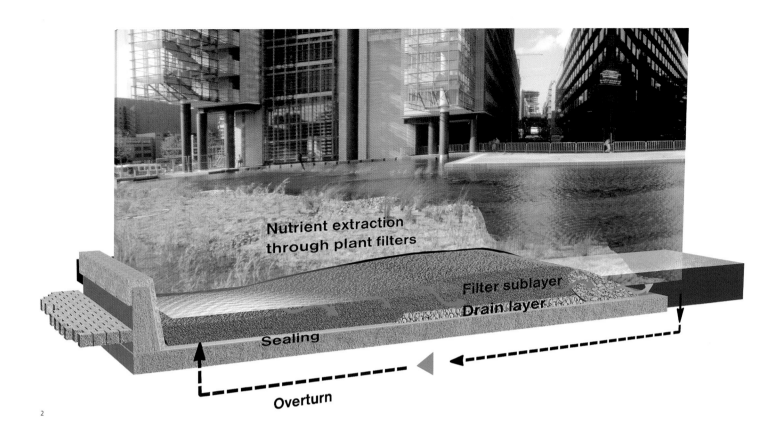

Nutrient extraction through plant filters

Filter sublayer

Drain layer

Sealing

Overturn

2

■ 1 Biotope section. 2 A diagram of sand-mineral substrate and aquatic plants. 3 Constructed on top of a traffic tunnel, the biotope is lined with a geomembrane. 4 Substrate consists of sand, zeolite, and lava rock for high permeability and nutrient-fixing capacity. 5 Since the biotope has low nutrient loads, potted plants are densely spaced in order to compensate for any related loss of plant material. 6 The collected stormwater is circulated within a public interactive open-air water feature.

3

4

5

6

On-Site Sewage Treatment System //

Andropogon Associates + Kieran Timberlake Associates +
Natural Systems International

In order to incorporate the school's Quaker philosophy – to be stewards of the Earth – the Sidwell Middle School addition treats sewage on-site with a series of biological processes. THE MULTIPLE MECHANISMS ARE INTEGRATED INTO BOTH THE LANDSCAPE AND ARCHITECTURE, AND LEVERAGED INTO A SYSTEM THAT ENHANCES THE CHARACTER AND OPERATION OF BOTH. Additionally, the system is visible to the students, serving as a sustainable education tool.

Biological processes are highly energy-efficient as they rely strictly on natural biodegradation and do not require extensive electrical input. Many conventional systems use significantly greater electrical inputs and produce greater quantities of sludge that must be removed off-site. Biological systems produce little sludge by comparison, but are generally slower and require a larger footprint. At Sidwell, the terraced wetland needed for biological processes is also used as a courtyard, outdoor classroom, and habitat with a diversity of plant species.

Compared to centralized systems that involve extensive collection infrastructure, on-site waste treatment systems require relatively little infrastructure investment. Additionally, effluent is readily available for on-site uses, such as irrigation and toilet flushing. In contrast, it is rarely cost-effective for a centralized system to recirculate effluent, and instead, its nutrient-rich effluent is discharged into nearby water bodies, often leading to increased eutrophication.

At Sidwell, the on-site waste and effluent flows tie the biological operations of architecture and landscape into a circular, mutually beneficial relationship. Sewage from the building is given primary treatment in an underground tank and then circulated through a series of terraced reed beds in the courtyard (sewage water is not accessible at the surface). Within the wetlands, microorganisms attached to the gravel planting media and plant roots provide an efficient breakdown of water contaminants. A trickle filter and sand filter provide further treatment. The system receives up to 3,000gal (11,356l) per day and has a residence time between four and six days. The high-quality outflow from the system is intended for reuse in the building to supply 100% of the water required for toilet flushing. During the wintertime, warm wastewater from the building will ensure that the wetlands never freeze, though their biology will slow down.

Stormwater runoff is directed to a rain garden and pond. Runoff from the roof is collected in an underground cistern, which is designed to maintain the water levels of the pond during dry weather. Water fills the rain garden during a storm and then slowly seeps into the ground, where it is naturally filtered by the soil. Excess rainwater in the cistern wells up from a millstone spring and flows to the pond. During a heavy rain, the pond will also overflow through a slotted weir into the rain garden. The dynamics of the changing water levels are a visible reflection of the local rainfall, cycling from wet to dry throughout the season.

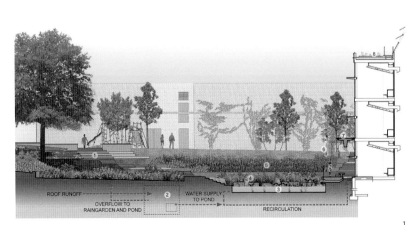

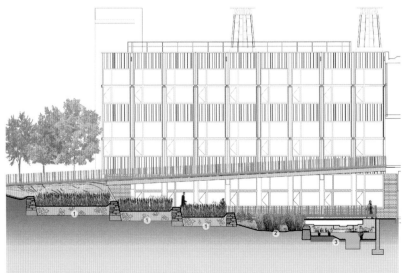

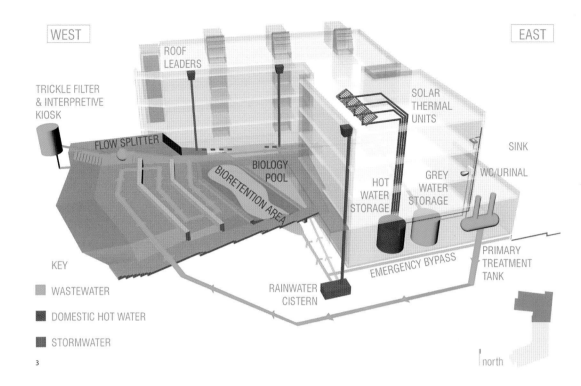

WEST | EAST

ROOF LEADERS

TRICKLE FILTER & INTERPRETIVE KIOSK

SOLAR THERMAL UNITS

FLOW SPLITTER

BIOLOGY POOL

SINK

BIORETENTION AREA

HOT WATER STORAGE

GREY WATER STORAGE

WC/URINAL

KEY

WASTEWATER

DOMESTIC HOT WATER

STORMWATER

RAINWATER CISTERN

EMERGENCY BYPASS

PRIMARY TREATMENT TANK

north

1 The wetland system treats sewage and grey water from the building. 2 Illustrated section of wetland treatment systems. 3 Diagram of the closed-loop water system. 4 Perspective visualization of terraced wetlands and new building.

3

4

In their design to reconfigure the shipyard landscape of Dock No.1 for Urban Outfitter's corporate offices, D.I.R.T. studio sought to reveal the traces of previous production at the former Philadelphia Navy Yard. INNOVATING THE USUAL "HOG-AND-HAUL" DEMOLITION APPROACH, D.I.R.T. STUDIO DEPLOYED A SALVAGING STRATEGY THAT DIGESTS THE "UNDESIRABLE DETRITUS" INTO A NOVEL REUSE.

D.I.R.T. studio initiated their intervention on-site with "site forensics", which were conceived as an examination process of the existing ground as a stratified surface. This process "unearthed" the Philadelphia Navy Yard's material palette, which consisted of sweeping lengths of rail tracks, stained expanses of concrete, rusted metal grates, and industrial residue.

The proposed technique to peel the existing conditions and reconstitute the site was in itself not new. However, this strategy of recycling and reusing on-site and in-situ materials posed difficulties for detailing and cost estimates. D.I.R.T. developed full-scale mock-up experiments as a tactic to gain contractor and client approval. A test trench was dug to reveal the existing constructed layers. LARGE PIECES OF BROKEN-UP CONCRETE WERE ARRANGED INTO A NEW PATTERN OF PAVING, WITH INTERSPERSED TREE PLANTING AND STONE DUST FILLING THE CREVICES. THE TECHNIQUE ACHIEVED THE REUSE OF 100% OF DEMOLITION DEBRIS THAT TYPICALLY ENDS UP IN A LANDFILL.

Reminiscent of the "Flintstones" cartoon television show; the D.I.R.T. studio coined the reuse of busted concrete pieces "Barney Rubble". The recipe calls for the following ingredients and preparations:

- ■ Remove bituminous veneer.
- ■ Break up the concrete into 2–4ft (0.6–1.2m) pieces.
- ■ Examine soils sub-grade for proper drainage and amend soil as necessary.
- ■ Lay out "puzzle" pieces "like painting your way out of a room".
- ■ Use skid steer to lower concrete chunks and manually shimmy them level onto existing grade.
- ■ Plant black locusts incrementally in-between a pattern of "busted" concrete pieces in tight two-foot clumps with open 10 or 12ft (3.7m) gaps.
- ■ Taper the depth around tree trunks.
- ■ And compact stone dust into the crevices.

■ **1** Sections showing the sequence of the construction process. **2** Existing ground. **3** Removing bituminous veneer. **4** Sorting through the pile of the concrete pieces. **5** Black Locusts are planted incrementally in between the concrete pieces. **6** Laying out 2–4ft (0.6–1.2m) concrete pieces. **7** Stone dust is compacted in the crevices.

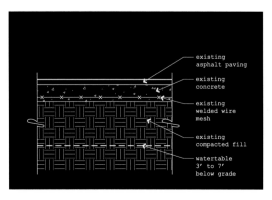

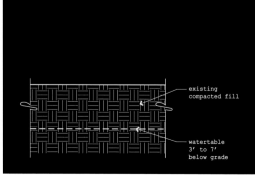

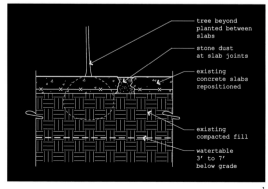

1

2

3

4

5

6

7

1

2

■ **1** Barney Rubble technique achieved the reuse of 100% of demolition debris that typically heads for a landfill. **2** Barney Rubble after installation.

Strategic Contaminated Soil Placement //
Gustafson Porter

In 1967, following 82 years of use as a central gas works, the site of Amsterdam's Westergasfabriek was in a condition unsuitable for public use. The process of extracting gas from coal had left the site with a host of toxic chemicals. In the 30-year interim between the site's industrial use and the current park, the polluted grounds and historic industrial buildings became a home for squatters and location for occasional legal and illicit cultural events. Initial remediation studies recommended a prohibitively expensive off-site disposal of the polluted soil, leaving the site in an indeterminate state.

In 2003, the Westergasfabriek Cultural Park opened without the removal of any polluted soil and has quickly become a popular and valued urban park, containing a wide variety of amenities. AT THE CORE OF THIS TRANSFORMATION IS AN ECONOMICAL AND MULTI-FACETED STRATEGY FOR COORDINATING PARK USE AND TOPOGRAPHY WITH THE PLACEMENT OF CONTAMINATED SOIL ON SITE.

With a site measuring 13ha (32ac), Westergasfabriek was Amsterdam's largest gas works. Following its closure, 19 industrial buildings remain on site, all of which are protected as historic structures under Dutch law, as well as a series of gas-holding tanks, tar pits and other processing structures. The site was heavily contaminated from the gas manufacturing process, when heavy metals, volatile organic compounds and benzene leached into the soil. Surveys showed that both the site's soil and ground water were heterogeneously contaminated with a cocktail of substances, ranging from cyanide to asbestos.

The Ministry of Housing, Spatial Planning, and the Environment agreed that the most cost-effective solution was to Isolate, Control, and Monitor (ICM) polluted soil on-site, a strategy that would cost approximately $1/6$ of what it would cost to remove the soil. The ISM strategy calls for a layer, usually an impenetrable surface such as asphalt, to cap the contaminated soil and prevent any exposure. However, besides the significant cost, applying such an impenetrable layer to the entire site has disadvantages. Primarily, a flat sheet of asphalt is an ill-suited topography upon which to build a verdant city park. Additionally, the structures on site were built on timber piles that could rot if the current water level was not maintained through regular rainfall infiltration. Prior to the landscape design of the park, engineers determined that it was better to tilt the impenetrable layer so that areas where the cap was at the surface could also serve as paving, while sunken areas served as a base to create the park's landscape and topography. At this point a standard percentage of park paving was determined as well as an amount of soil that would have to be moved within the site.

Even after adopting the ICM strategy the remediation costs were too high. The remediation engineers further reduced costs with the discovery that one meter of clean soil could serve as an isolation layer, as long as it was placed where the contaminated ground water could not rise high enough to contaminate the clean layer of soil. This technique eliminated the necessity for a continuous and costly impenetrable layer and allowed the isolation layer to be primarily composed of planting soil with a thin substrata membrane divider. It also allowed water to infiltrate and maintain the integrity of the buildings' timber foundations. The impenetrable layer was reserved for spaces below the high-water mark and where park circulation or program dictated a hard surface.

Following the combined tilt and ISM strategy, topography was created by the carefully balanced cut and fill of contaminated soils. Soil was cut from the area around the buildings and the excavation of the canal, where paving would be placed. The contaminated soil that was covered with clean soil and contoured such that the placement of the clean soil, with depths required for the different plant types (e.g. trees vs. grass), would result in a smooth topography, hiding the artificial condition below and economizing the use of clean soil. Some existing mature trees were preserved by carefully digging out a certain depth of contaminated soil around the roots and replacing the contaminated soil with clean soil.

MUCH OF THE SUCCESS OF WESTERGASFABRIEK CULTURAL PARK LIES WITHIN A STRATEGY OF ECONOMY AND COORDINATION BETWEEN THE PARK DESIGN AND SITE REMEDIATION STRATEGY. The strategy allows for the careful internal manipulation of contaminated soil into a complex system that serves multiple operational goals as well as creating an attractive topographical landscape. However, the success and seamlessness of the park's surfaces may be a lost opportunity to register this layering that could continue to educate people about the site's industrial legacy, one that does not only remain in the historic buildings, but also within the site's horizons.

■ **1** The site was heavily contaminated from the gas manufacturing process. **2** Cut and fill areas.

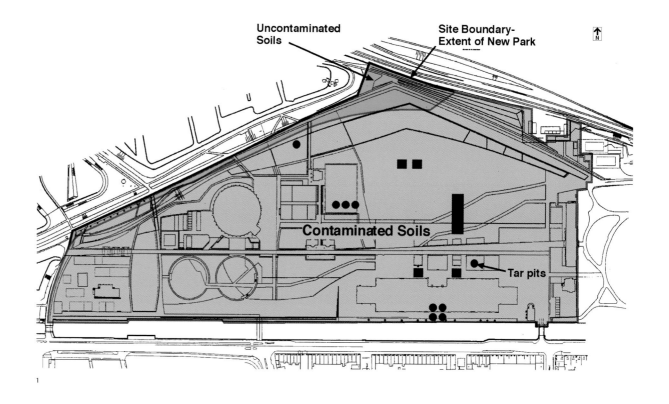

1

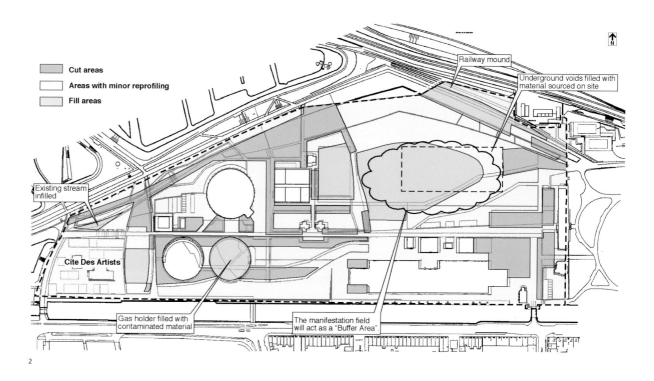

2

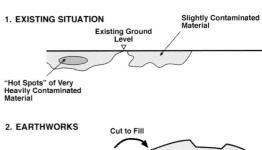

1. EXISTING SITUATION

Existing Ground Level

Slightly Contaminated Material

"Hot Spots" of Very Heavily Contaminated Material

2. EARTHWORKS

Cut to Fill

Hot Spots Removed

3. PLACEMENT OF ISOLATION LAYER

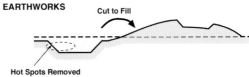

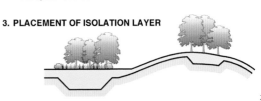

Existing Tree

Uncontaminated Soil

Topsoil (Clean)

Subsoil (Clean)

Geotextile

Existing Trees - Contaminated Areas

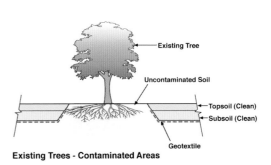

Existing Tree

Contaminated soil dug out by hand - Replaced with clean topsoils

Topsoil (Clean)

Subsoil (Clean)

Geotextile

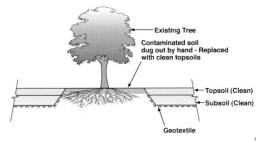

5

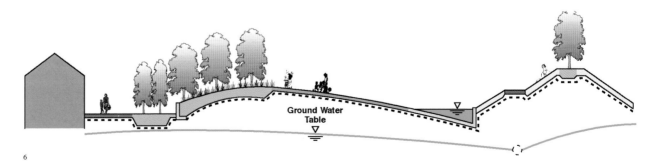

1 Aerial photograph during the construction period showing the cut and fill siteworks. **2** Earthworks strategy. **3** Soil placement corresponds with the layout of wetlands, trails, and railroad berm. **4** Strategy for preserving existing trees. **5** Park recreational program is distributed in relation to the strategies of contaminated soil cut and fill. **6** Soil and paving was distributed above the contaminated soil according to vegetation type and use.

Ground Water Table

6

■ Translate

TRANSLATE IS THE MERGING OF LANDSCAPE AND COMMUNICATION: AN EVOLVING REPRESENTATION OF LOCAL AND CONTEXTUAL CONDITIONS. HERE, DATA IS CONSIDERED AS A LIVING SYSTEM. THIS CHAPTER INVESTIGATES THE MATERIALIZATION OF DATA SYSTEMS IN THE LANDSCAPE, AND FOCUSES ON NUMERICAL ATTRIBUTES OF A SINGLE OR SET OF DYNAMIC FORCES AND SITE PROPERTIES.

From cellular technologies to the infinite Internet web of information, real-time communication and universal data streams have become increasingly integrated into our everyday environments. Satellite transmission, photo documentation, fiber optics, and smart technologies are commonly inserted into daily consumer products including wearables, architecture, and transportation. In a similar vein, landscape architecture has been engaged in site and non-site data gathering due to increased interest in assessing systems in flux: hurricanes, earthquakes, and toxic conditions among others. Following groundbreaking precedents in science and ecology as well as utility infrastructure, monitoring and detection processes have become integral tools for landscape architects to not only communicate site conditions, but also to dictate program and visual space.

Translate is the merging of landscape and communication: an evolving representation of local and contextual conditions. Here, data is considered as a Living System. This chapter investigates the materialization of data systems in the landscape, and focuses on numerical attributes of a single or set of dynamic forces and site properties. Whether obtained remotely or from on-site sensors, these measurements are synthesized, decoded, evaluated, and interpreted into various forms of communication and responsive structures.

Translate fits within the current dialogue concerning the didactic value and potential of landscape design: design that seeks to form meaning or contemporary insight in regard to environmental, political, socio-economic, or professional contexts.

The projects included in this chapter aim to educate visitors and provide information through interactive and reactive sets of feedback operations.

As global and regional occurrences impact the local site (weather, pollution, movement, noise, urban processes), Translate presents interpretive representational methods that elucidate and describe both invisible conditions and occurrences over time. In addition, Translate is considered to be an act of conversion. This can manifest in operations like energy harvesting that use sources ranging from the motion of pedestrians or vehicles to solar energy, tidal waves, or wind forces collected through mechanical devices and adapted to operate the site. Combining sensor/digital and mechanical devices, Translate systems detect compound signals to gauge mutable site conditions, or absorb energy to convert into new performances.

The Fiber Optic Marsh establishes a monitoring system for a coastal marsh restoration. Constructed of sensing and illuminating fiber optics, the matrix is engineered as an alternative to eelgrass habitat while constantly measuring pollution levels in the water. Once collected, pollution data is translated into a range of glowing colors to communicate water quality. At night, the Fiber Optic Marsh creates a spectacular data-driven light show, shifting as tides and pollution go through states of flux. The marsh then becomes a didactic tool to illuminate visitors and park managers of the otherwise hidden levels of pollution.

AS GLOBAL AND REGIONAL OCCURRENCES IMPACT THE LOCAL SITE (WEATHER, POLLUTION, MOVEMENT, NOISE, URBAN PROCESSES), TRANSLATE PRESENTS INTERPRETIVE REPRESENTATIONAL METHODS THAT ELUCIDATE AND DESCRIBE BOTH INVISIBLE CONDITIONS AND OCCURRENCES OVER TIME.

The Besòs River Weather Informed Park Access System informs and controls park access in accordance with weather and hydrologic information. A central system gathers local and regional weather patterns and interprets emergency flood conditions to control park access via digital LED signage dispersed throughout the park. This responsive signage effectively expands the site's performance by enabling the flood zone to serve as a large-scale open space amenity.

Courtyard in the Wind harnesses wind force and converts it into electrical power to operate the movement of a courtyard surface. Situated on a circular track with an embedded motor, the entire landscape, including trees, bench, paving, and visitors rotate as if on a turntable. Referencing the potential of energy harvesting in the landscape, wind forces here are automated into a mechanical landscape performance. The landscape is activated solely with the energy produced from available on-site resources, which would otherwise flow unobserved.

The Olympic Park in Athens deploys dozens of sound and motion sensors throughout the site to detect the rush and vibrancy of thousands of visitors who attend the games throughout day and night. The data collected is computed and animated into the pneumatic movement of a giant figurative sculpture. In effect, the sculpture communicates the hum and roars of the audience in real-time by changing its shape and color. Several permutations of motion and colors represent various modes of excitement, sound, and frequency.

In the product section, Data Fountain exemplifies a merging between landscape, media, and message. The system draws its data from current global news and financial information. A computer program translates the relative data, which is then used to control and determine the display of a fountain and the intensity of the projected water.

Sandscape & Illuminating Clay was developed as a landscape design tool that integrates physical modelmaking with real-time computational analysis. As the designer manually models the terrain in clay or sand, the changing geometry is captured real-time by a sensing technology. The data is transformed into a digital elevation model as well as a series of Geographic Information System (GIS) analysis maps (slope, solar aspect, water flow, and shadows), which are then projected back onto the landscape model. The whole interaction loop happens in one second per cycle. Data and form are generated within the same space, each informing the other. Design and advanced analysis become a real-time process and incorporate precision into the fluid process of modeling the landscape.

Pneumatic Body //
ONL [Oosterhuis_Lénárd]

A proposed pavilion by architects ONL for the Athens Olympic Games, Pneumatic Body was conceived as an interactive landmark that is activated by the flux of fans and visitors. STANDING 30M (98.5FT) TALL IN THE MIDST OF THE OLYMPIC PARK, THE PNEUMATIC TENSILE STRUCTURE GAUGES THE ACTIVITY AND EXCITEMENT OF PARTICIPANTS, VISITORS AND FANS AND TRANSLATES VOLUME AND FREQUENCY INTO AN ANATOMICAL FIGURE IN MOTION. By visualizing the soundscape and movement of visitors throughout the park over the course of the day "the collective becomes aware of its own behavior, its own influence".

Throughout the Olympic Park, dispersed Agents record local and remote spatial and aural events and transmit signals to the Body via embedded wireless sensors. "From a collective hum to roar" the Body reacts in real-time by transforming its shape and color. Constructed of a matrix of pneumatic tubes, called Fluidic Muscles. The body produces multiple gestures reminescent of extended or flexed arms and legs. Manufactured by Festo, the Fluidic Muscles are actuators with a pressure-sealed rubber tube encased in a three-dimensional textile mesh. The Body's skin is made of a translucent elastomeric polymer, accentuated in colors resembling the hues of the rings of the Olympic games. An internally mounted light system illuminates the body at night, while an animated display LED matrix displays information.

The Fluid Muscles are individually controlled via magnetic valves, which are programmed by a processing unit. The software Virtools, which is typically used for interactive game-design, is used to script the behavior profiles of the Body. Linked to a high-pressure air distribution device, the software translates sounds and movement signals into air pressure levels. As internal pressure is applied, the tube expands, creating a tensile force and a contraction motion in the Muscle's longitudinal direction, which causes the elastomeric skin to stretch in multiple directions. Consequently, the Body's multiple arms kick, punch, and exclaim triumphantly.

■ **1** The Pneumatic Body structure has multiple levels of excitement: a bored-lonely dance, hype, and panic. **2** The shape, color, and motion of the Pneumatic Body is a real-time reaction to the flux of the masses.

1

2

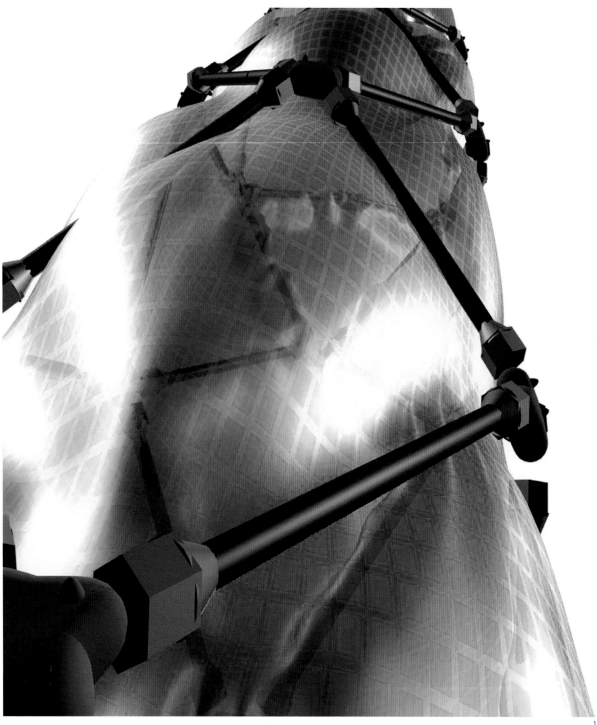

■ **1** The Body's skin is made of a translucent elastomeric polymer with an internally mounted LED light display. **2** The Pneumatic Body expresses the sound and movement throughout the Olympic site. **3** Festo Fluidic Muscles are pneumatic actuators that allow for the expansion and contraction of deployable structures. **4** Monitoring devices register signals of activity and transmit them to the Pneumatic Body.

1

2

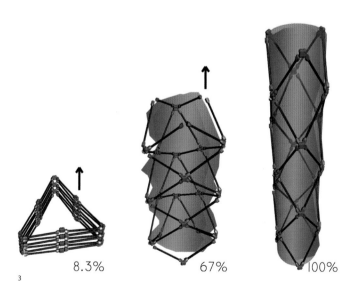

8.3%   67%   100%

3

4

Powered by Wind, the Ground is a Turntable //

Acconci Studio + Wolfgang Hermann Niemeyer

Courtyard in the Wind, Buildings Department Administration Building,
Munich, Germany

Wind energy is translated into the unlikely rotation of a mechanical platform embedded in the courtyard of Munich's building department administrative building. A turbine placed atop the building tower captures wind energy that is used to power a turntable of landscape, lying within the protected confines of the building's walls. A connection, however abstract and perhaps invisible, is made between the force of wind and the slow rotation of the platform. The effect of this unlikely relationship is a surreal and unprecedented landscape condition: A PORTION OF A COMMON COURTYARD DESIGN BECOMES A MOVING IMAGE OF CONSTRUCTED NATURE, WHERE TREES, PAVING, LIGHTING, AND BENCHES ALIKE REVOLVE AS IF ON DISPLAY.

The rotating ring of landscape in Acconci Studio's Courtyard In The Wind rests flush with the surrounding lawn and paved courtyard. The turntable contains all the typical landscape components, creating an illusion of continuity between the trees, grass, and paved areas of the formal courtyard, if only for one moment in its revolu-

tions. As the ring rotates, this composition revolves in and out of alignment, carrying trees and visitors alike. Building occupants around the courtyard are presented with a view of a seemingly normal composition performing a mechanical dance. The turntable is designed to act as a massive mobile planter. It rotates on a track contained in a sub-surface circular chamber that houses a set of motors and series of wheels. The wind turbine, mounted on the tower, generates the energy used by the motors to rotate the wheels. With a rotation frequency of two revolutions per hour, the landscape moves slowly, at about 2 cm/sec. At this speed the movement is barely visually perceptible and can be slightly felt by visitors walking across the turntable.

WHILE NOT A DIRECT "TRANSLATION" OF WIND INTENSITY, NOR A MEASUREMENT OF ITS DIRECTIONALITY, THE MANIFESTATION OF THE WIND ON THE COURTYARD LANDSCAPE GIVES FORM AND EXPERIENCE TO THE INTANGIBLE FORCE OF WIND.

1 The rotating ring of landscape rests flush with the surrounding lawn and paved courtyard. **2** As the ring rotates, this composition revolves in and out of alignment, carrying trees and visitors alike. **3** A turbine placed atop the building tower captures wind energy that is used to rotate its inner courtyard. **4** Plans of the foundation, footing, and rotating ring.

1

2

3

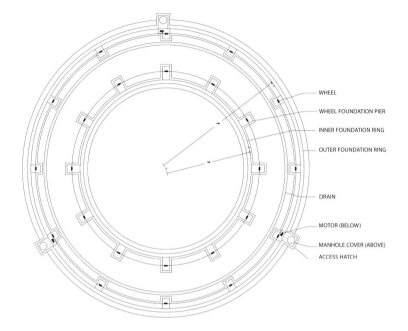

WHEEL

WHEEL FOUNDATION PIER

INNER FOUNDATION RING

OUTER FOUNDATION RING

DRAIN

MOTOR (BELOW)

MANHOLE COVER (ABOVE)

ACCESS HATCH

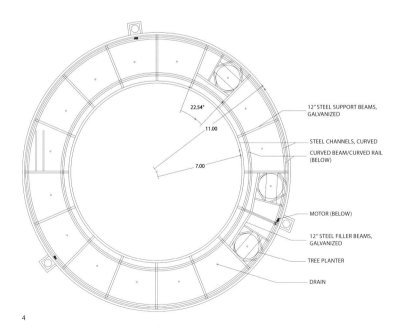

22.54°

11.00

7.00

12" STEEL SUPPORT BEAMS,
GALVANIZED

STEEL CHANNELS, CURVED

CURVED BEAM/CURVED RAIL
(BELOW)

MOTOR (BELOW)

12" STEEL FILLER BEAMS,
GALVANIZED

TREE PLANTER

DRAIN

4

Weather Informed Park Access System //
Barcelona Regional, Agència Metropolitana de Desenvolupament
Urbanístic i d'Infraestructures S.A.

Environmental Restoration of Besòs River Barcelona, Spain

In 1962, a catastrophic flood of Barcelona's Rio Besòs caused about 800 casualties and extensive property damage. To prevent further catastrophe, the river walls were reinforced with 4m (13ft) high concrete walls containing the 130 m (426.5 ft) wide channel. As such, the system was effective as a flood management device, but otherwise became an infrastructural eyesore. Damaged by pollution and strained by a growing city, the river consequently became increasingly abused and neglected. The 1996 Environmental Restoration of Besòs River recognized that the future success of the river relied on the active use and stewardship of its neighbors and created a plan to allow users safe access to open space inside widened areas of the highly volatile river channel.

Because of the arid climate, the fluvial park is serene and safe for most of the year; however, during storms torrential rains create flows that rapidly reach levels dangerous for park users in the channel. In these conditions access must be monitored by a predictive system, to forewarn users prior to a torrential storm. To accomplish this, Barcelona Regional devised a smart access system: Storm Surge Warning System (SAHBE). A central control center, located 15km (9.3mi) from the park, uses a macro-computing model to synchronize park access with weather conditions. The model synthesizes multiple data sources, including hydrological data collected by river-wide sensors, satellite, weather radar information, and video footage captured from cameras placed along the river-banks. The resultant model consequently controls the river's 19 access points. Each set of stairs and ramp, leading down to the park in the flood plain, is furnished with manually controlled gates and digitally operated LED (light emitting diodes) message signs. Four agents staff the park throughout the day solely for the purpose of assisting people and ensuring that safety precautions are followed. Sirens and loudspeakers further amplify the emergency status for users inside the channel.

The SAHBE system exemplifies a park that is responsive to its weather context. THE SYSTEM RECOGNIZES THE EFFICIENCY OF CHANGING ACCESS OF USERS, RATHER THAN CHANGING TOPOGRAPHICAL OR FLUVIAL CONDITIONS. BY PROVIDING EMERGENCY INFORMATION TO THE PARK'S USERS, THE RIVER IS EFFECTIVELY TRANSFORMED FROM A POTENTIALLY HAZARDOUS INFRASTRUCTURE INTO A VALUABLE REGIONAL AMENITY. While such remote information systems are often employed on highways, few have been employed effectively to help users interact with other complex infrastructural conditions. Thus, there is still a great potential for the integration of interactive, informative, and responsive signage in park design.

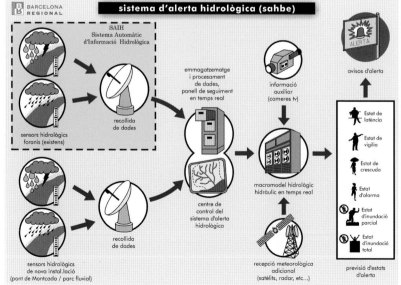

1

2

1 During rain events stormwater rises up the channel walls, submerging the fluvial parks. **2** SAHBE synthesizes hydrological data collected by river-wide sensors, satellite and weather radar information, and video footage of the river-banks. **3** An LED sign declares that access to the river is restricted. **4** The 19 access points include stairs, ramps, and manually controlled gates.

3

4

Fiber Optic Marsh //
Abby Feldman, Harvard University, Graduate School of Design

At night, the water off the coastline of Providence's Field's Point glows with a shifting array of luminescent colors. Bundles of fiber optics, connected through an anchored matrix of conduits, sway with the tidal flux. Fitted to monitor pollution levels in the water, the fiber optic strands translate the data into a dynamic pixilated painting. Fish now dwell in this constructed habitat, consuming marine organisms attached to the synthetic infrastructure.

THE FIBER OPTIC MARSH PROPOSES A HYBRID OF TWO LIVING SYSTEMS: A STRUCTURAL SYSTEM THAT ENABLES THE ESTABLISHMENT OF DEVASTATED EELGRASS MARSH ECOLOGY IN HIGHLY POLLUTED COASTAL ENVIRONMENTS; AND A SENSORY SYSTEM THAT ILLUMINATES DATA, BOTH LITERALLY AND FIGURATIVELY.

The fiber optic bundles are proposed to act as an aquatic infrastructure initiating a new food chain and habitat where eelgrass marshes once thrived. This artificial solution is a response to eutrophication, caused by excessive nutrient quantities in the water (primarily phosphorus, nitrogen, and carbon) due to urban runoff and sewage plant effluents. This condition has a ripple effect: excess nutrients in the water lead to an increase of algae, which prevent ultraviolet light from penetrating the water's surface. Consequently, essential epiphytic plants, microorganisms and eelgrasses cannot thrive, breaking the food chain and resulting in the disappearance of marine and wildlife habitat. To restart such a complex and intricate coastal ecology after its destruction is difficult. Hence, there is a need for a synthetic launcher.

The proposed use of synthetic fibers relies on the assumption that epiphytes merely require a surface area to attach to, but that this surface need not be a plant material. Once established, the epiphytic microorganisms can metabolize nutrients and contaminants, reversing the effects of eutrophication, improving the water quality and enabling natural vegetation to take root. The synthetic marsh can also be constructed as a transitional system, with biodegradable polymer fiber optics, which degrade over a determined period of time. In addition, the conduit matrix that houses the fiber optic bundles can act as an erosion control structure reinforcing coastal banks until plant roots re-establish themselves.

Fiber optic bundles are to be spaced with enough density for good color retention. They must be end-emitting fibers, and selected for a specific level of attenuation depending on the required level of luminosity. The strands are highly efficient, do not produce heat, and do not emit ultraviolet or infrared rays.

THE MARSH IS A VISUAL TRANSLATION WHICH MAKES THE CONDITION OF THE AQUATIC ECOLOGY LEGIBLE, WHERE EMITTED LIGHT TRANSFORMS THE WATER INTO A NIGHTTIME SPECTACLE.

1

2

3

1 Fiber optic bundles provide the surface area for algae and fish habitat. 2 The conduit matrix can act as an erosion control structure. 3 Programmed to monitor pollution levels in the water, the fiber optic strands translate data into dynamic luminosity. 4 The Fiber Optic Marsh enables the re-establishment of eelgrass marsh ecology in highly polluted coastal environments.

4

Volatile

MOMENTARY, DAILY AND SEASONAL CYCLES OF EPHEMERAL FORCES SUCH AS WIND, RAIN, FOG, CLOUDS, LIGHT, SOUND, AND TEMPERATURE ANIMATE THE LANDSCAPE WITH A VAST ARRAY OF EXPERIENTIAL CONDITIONS. THESE ATMOSPHERIC PHENOMENA DEFINE OUR IMMERSED EXPERIENCE OF A SITE; YET DO SO WITHOUT OCCUPYING ARCHITECTONIC SPACE.

At once ordinary, elemental, and volatile, weather phenomena are often the most beguiling and intangible sets of processes within the landscape. Momentary, daily, and seasonal cycles of ephemeral forces such as wind, rain, fog, clouds, light, sound, and temperature animate the landscape with a vast array of experiential conditions. These atmospheric phenomena define our immersed experience of a site; yet do so without occupying architectonic space.

Volatile considers the immateriality of atmospheric phenomena and how weather dynamism can be conceived of as a tectonic landscape experience. Volatile questions how substances without form can be technically constructed and specified, and how structures and technologies control, create, and shape such uncontrollable systems to create artificial and choreographed weather.

From wind walls to misting pergolas, and from artificial clouds to digitally animated rain, these staged performances are reminders of the processes that order the landscape on a macro scale; they reference larger pervasive patterns that operate globally but activate the immediate site. The selected projects focus on methods that reproduce, describe, and highlight these volatile patterns onsite: to emphasize their multiple phases and their auditory, optical, and kinesthetic properties over time.

In this chapter, the choreography of weather brings forth the issue of the spectacle in the landscape. Volatile seeks to stage a poetic performance of sensorial dynamism by reframing and visualizing fleeting and ethereal effects.

The Weather Garden sets up a stage solely for the atmospheric impressions of rain puddles. The stone surface of the courtyard is modeled to capture rainwater in a pattern of puddles. While the puddles evaporate at different rates, they transform into an animated performance of morphing shapes that reflect the sky's moving clouds and shifting light.

Ned Kahn's Wind Wall visually registers the extreme complexity and volatility of wind patterns. Despite its ubiquitous presence and our familiarity with the sensorial effects of wind as it whistles, rustles, and blows the leaves on a tree, the actual patterns of turbulence and eddies are often invisible. Composed of grids of thousands of rotating metal squares or pixels that fluctuate in the wind, the facade acts as a canvas for the visualization of the intricate flow patterns, much like a sand dune shaped by the desert wind. In addition, the porous wall serves as an effective shade to filter light transmission and regulate interior climate.

Volatile also investigates the issue of the technological/digital sublime and the intersection between media and weather. It explores the methods by which a weather phenomenon is recreated, regulated, monitored, and adjusted to respond to external conditions and program input.

Pitterpatterns features a computerized rainfall as a building façade. Traditional landscapes and architectural structures are built to resist and protect against natural elements; here, a weather system is integrated into the building façade. A cantilevered artificial "cloud" defines the threshold experience, but blurs the distinc-

VOLATILE QUESTIONS HOW SUBSTANCES WITHOUT FORM CAN BE TECHNICALLY CONSTRUCTED AND SPECIFIED, AND HOW STRUCTURES AND TECHNOLOGIES CONTROL, CREATE, AND SHAPE SUCH UNCONTROLLABLE SYSTEMS TO CREATE ARTIFICIAL AND CHOREOGRAPHED WEATHER.

tion between the conventional perception of outside and inside. Each rain nozzle in the cantilevered roof is controlled by software capable of creating any variety of spatial and temporal patterns or "rainformations". The digital compositions produce a fully sensorial experience of a passage through a rainfall soundscape, a cooler microclimate, as well as an illuminated spectacle at night.

In Pink Cloud, Harvey Milk is memorialized with an artificially colored cloud that floats over a street intersection in San Francisco. The cloud is generated with artificial fog-making technology that adapts to the fog patterns of San Francisco. Sensing when clouds are absent, a series of poles emits a fine spray, and fog hovers over the intersection. The artificial cloud is also designed to be interactive, allowing visitors to activate the cloud using a coin-operated meter. The Responsive Cloud Machine effectively reverses the usual permanence of memorial materiality with an ephemeral spectacle that is refreshingly expressive of whimsy and impermanence. Its ethereal iconography is fleeting, yet monumental.

The pergola in Parque de Diagonal Mar, featured in the Launch chapter, vaporizes water into mist to cool the air on a hot Barcelona day, and to mimic the atmosphere of the nearby ocean shorefront.

The Bamboo Garden in Erie Street Plaza, featured in the Grooming chapter, generates hot steam during winter. Bamboo planters are embedded with pumps which draw and convert groundwater into steam to create a warm microclimate and a mysterious dreamscape against the backdrop of a snowy Wisconsin landscape.

Responsive Cloud Machine //
Christian Werthmann & LOMA architecture.landscape.urbanism

Harvey Milk Memorial, San Francisco, California, USA

PINK CLOUD IS A "RESPONSIVE WEATHER MACHINE" THAT REACTS TO THE DAILY ENCROACHMENT OF THE SAN FRANCISCO FOG CLIMATE. The cloud was conceived as a memorial to honor Harvey Milk, a gay rights activist and first publicly known homosexual to serve on the city council of an American city, who was shot to death along with Mayor George Moscone in 1978 by a fellow councilman. In 2000 Christian Werthmann & LOMA won the competition for the Harvey Milk Memorial with a design that "challenges traditional concepts of memorialization". An artificially generated cloud was proposed as an immaterial alternative "where stone or bronze was the default material to fight against the erosion of memory".

Hovering over the intersection of Market Street in the Castro, directly above six lanes of traffic and 50,000 cars per day, the Cloud is not only a weather event, but also a dreamscape that declares the cultural dynamism of the Castro, the gay neighborhood of San Francisco.

The Cloud is produced with a fog machine, a common technology used in stage events. The fog is composed of a glycol-water mix that can vary in density. The mix is heated to about 200 – 300°F (93.3 – 148.9°C) and converted into vapor. Upon contact with cool air the vapor goes through a condensation phase to form a dense fog that when sprayed can reach a distance of 40ft (12.2m). Werthmann & LOMA investigated a variety of "cloud making" techniques, such as the fabrication of large-scale rain clouds in arid zones, steam generation, and theatrical special effects such as dry ice, as well as pyrotechnics. Many of those technologies involved massive infrastructure and energy, with adverse effects such as rain, haze, or carbon dioxide. These ephemeral effects were also studied for their duration, dimensional coverage, scattering and dissipating behavior, particularly in response to the daily weather dynamics. The most effective technology turned out to be the common fog machine.

The proposal calls for two or three 30ft (9.1m) high poles to be placed at each intersection corner. The fog machine sits in a sub-ground chamber and pumps the glycol-water mix up to a spray nozzle located at the tip of each pole. Activated in unison, the poles emit fog and form the Cloud. Pole-mounted light fixtures illuminate the Cloud in a variety of colors. ALWAYS VARYING IN FORM DUE TO THE FORCE OF WINDS, THE CLOUD IS ALSO INTENDED AS AN INTERACTIVE PIECE, CONTROLLED BY VISITORS VIA A COIN-OPERATED DEVICE OR VIA WIRELESS CELLULAR COMMUNICATION.

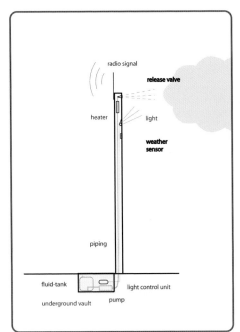

radio signal

release valve

heater

light

weather sensor

piping

fluid-tank

light control unit

underground vault

pump

light system
Integrated below the release valves. The light machine is using the combination of color and pattern with a motorized color wheel with 13 interchangeable colors and continuous scroll effect. A powerful 250W discharge lamp and a highly efficient reflector give a forceful beam of light.

underground vault
Each pole is supported by equipment installed in a nearby underground vault. This easy accessible shaft contains the tank with the fluid, pump and the light control unit.

central-steering-unit
Programmed to filter information from individual weather sensors, the steering and lightsystem sending a condition signal to the City department.

central-control-unit
Managing incoming information and error-handling. The control unit is turning the fog-machines off/on and gives commands to the light unit according to prepro-grammed scenarios.

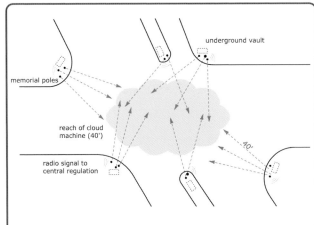

underground vault

memorial poles

reach of cloud machine (40')

radio signal to central regulation

40'

weather sensor
Constantly changing wheather conditions including air pressure, temperature and wind are registered and transfered by the weather sensor timing the appearance of the cloud above the crossing.

city department
Wireless "on the road" contact to the steering and the central control unit.

1

2

1 The fog machine sits in a sub-ground chamber and pumps the glycol-water mix up to a spray nozzle located at the tip of each pole. Six 30ft (9.1m) high poles are to be placed at each intersection corner. 2 Pink Cloud is not only a weather event, but also a dreamscape that declares the cultural dynamism of the Castro, the gay neighborhood of San Francisco. 3 Elevation of Pink Cloud monument.

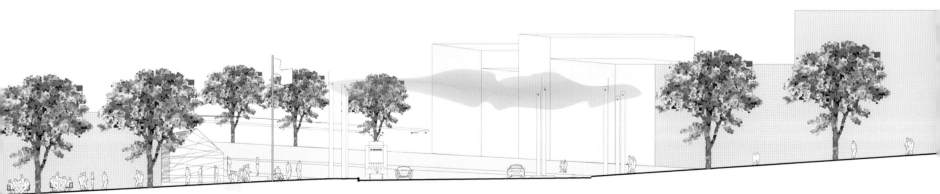

Harvey Milk Pavilion

3

▦ Computer Animated Rain //
J. MAYER H. Architekten

Pitterpatterns, Stadt.haus, Scharnhauser Park, Stuttgart, Germany

Pitterpatterns is an artificial rain device embedded in the facade of the Stuttgart municipal center. Computer-controlled rain emits from a cantilevered roof, placed like an architectonic cloud over the entrance of the building. **CONTRARY TO TYPICAL BUILDING ENVELOPES, PITTERPATTERNS EXPOSES THE ARCHITECTURE TO A WEATHER SYSTEM, BUT CONTROLLING IT TO CREATE EPHEMERAL EFFECTS AND DEFINE SPACE.** The normally volatile impact of weather becomes a controlled event that operates on the exterior of the building, the adjacent Market Square and the surrounding landscaped space.

The cantilevered roof, or cloud, houses a water tank and a filter system to treat collected rainwater. Cleansed stormwater is pumped out to a series of pipes, embedded in the cantilever, where two hundred openings are controlled by Pitterpatterns' computer software.

The system's software is programmed to emit rain in a variety of rhythms and compositions that transform the building's gateway into a meteorologically dynamic condition. Instant shifts in its settings can change the rain system to affect microclimate, building access, sound-scapes, and visual effects. The rain pattern can reflect or respond to contextual conditions ranging from meteorological to anthropomorphic.

These "rainformations", Mayer states, "question our understanding of natural and artificial weather conditions." He debunks the preconceived idea of Nature as naturally occurring and demonstrates the constructed and technological materiality of natural systems, particularly in the context of built landscape in the city. Computer-controlled rain patterns employ a set of ubiquitous digital imagery, such as the bar code or the digital clock, to evoke the idea of nature as technology.

1

2

1 Computer-controlled rain emits from a cantilevered roof.
2 200 openings in the pipes are synchronized to open and close according to Pitterpatterns' computer software.

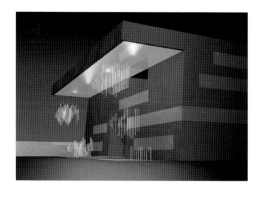

falling clouds

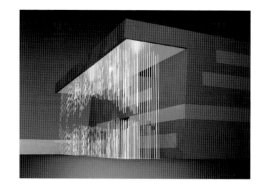

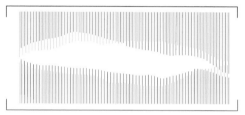

rain cave

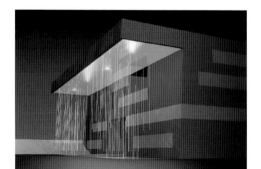

frequency shower

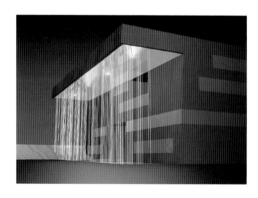

rain code

1

140

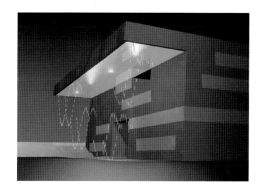

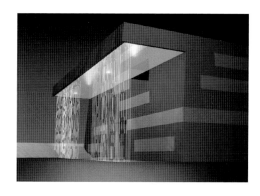

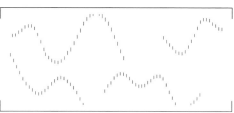

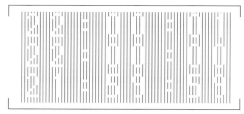

1 The patterns show a set of digital imagery such as a bar code or a digital clock, to evoke the idea of nature as technology.

sinus drops

time gaps

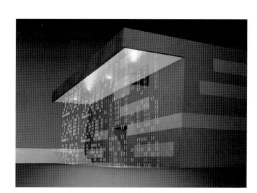

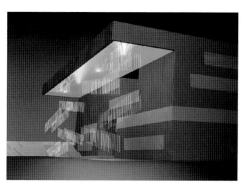

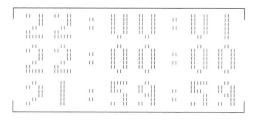

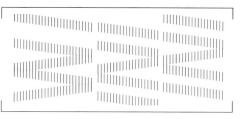

time drops

zig zag

1

Dynamic Thermal Wind Wall //
Ned Kahn

Wind Veil, Mesa Arts Center, Mesa, Arizona, USA
and **Technorama Façade,** Winterthur, Switzerland

Wind apparati usually manifest single measurements of wind: presence, vector, or intensity, and simplify our perception of the force. Only rarely, across a meadow field or amidst a flurry of papers do we gain a greater vision of the dynamism and complexity of wind patterns; of their ripples and vortices; sublime and volatile phenomena that even modern physics and mechanics has difficulty explaining. Ned Kahn's kinetic shade screens visually translate the beauty of this living force via a much more sensitive tool. This body of work employs compositions of simple elements to create an appropriate medium for natural forces to play their dynamic spectacle. Kahn considers his wind walls "detectors" analogous to detectors on telescopes and other devices that "reveal the effects of the invisible".

The Technorama façade is covered with 80,000 wind-animated panels. Each brushed aluminum panel is mounted on low-friction hinges so that the kinetic energy produced by wind easily animates these pixels. The dazzling patterns of this pixilated vision of the wind are further enhanced by the reflective quality of the panels. THE FAÇADE BECOMES A HYBRID OF SKY, LIGHT, AND WIND, DISSOLVING THE BUILDING INTO THE LANDSCAPE, AND CONVERTING A SOLID BUILDING SKIN INTO AN AMORPHOUS AND LIQUID-LIKE SUBSTANCE. The façade also becomes a living exhibit of the wind turbulence caused by the building. It should be noted that photographs cannot capture the startling speed and sensitivity to wind of the panels (captured best on film).

The kinetic wind walls at the Mesa Art Center differ from the Technorama in their aesthetic complexity and their operative potential in the desert climate. The smaller of the two screens further hybridizes wind with a vision of landscape by perforating the 9in (22.9cm) panels with a photographic pattern of sand dunes. The reflec-

tion of the environment is layered over subtle patterns of sand dune. The second panel tries a different hybrid approach. Blue-anodized 3in (7.6cm) aluminum panels are meant to create an illusion of a building submerged into "vertical water".

BOTH SCREENS WERE ALSO DESIGNED TO REDUCE SOLAR GAIN IN THE LOBBY OF THE BUILDING. THE SCREENS ARE PLACED 3FT (0.9M) FROM THE GLASS CURTAIN WALL TO ALLOW NATURAL AIR CURRENTS TO COOL THE BUILDING. AS THE SHINGLES WARM IN THE SUN, THEY CREATE CONVECTIVE AIR CURRENTS, WHICH DRAW COOLING AIR UP AGAINST THE GLASS. As a whole the screens are 50% open, allowing the transmission of air as well as light, lighting the lobby space with a phenomenological volatility of the wind and reducing cooling requirements by as much as 30% at some times of the year. Furthermore the fluttering of blue panels may also create a psychological effect of cooling.

One can draw many parallels with these structures and other landscape strategies as sophisticated means of harnessing the phenomenological characteristics of natural processes. The visual system combines two complex forces, ambient reflected light and wind patterns, to create a new and glittering spectacle. The success of this hybrid begs the question of what other forces might be hybridized to great effect; what else can index the volatility of wind or other natural forces? As a hybrid of forces the system also excels operationally as an enhanced transparent cooling screen, operationally blurring the boundaries between landscape and architecture. As a vertical landscape, these screens explore a realm relatively uncontested compared to the ground, but increasingly valued in dense urban conditions.

1

2

1 The Technorama façade is covered with 80,000 wind-animated panels. **2** Blue-anodized 3in (7.6cm) aluminum panels of the Mesa Arts Center Wind Veil are meant to create an illusion of a building submerged into "vertical water". **3** Each brushed aluminum panel is mounted on low-friction hinges so that the kinetic energy produced by wind easily animates these pixels. **4** Detail of Mesa Wind Veil.

3

4

1

2

1, 2 The screen is also designed to reduce solar gain inside the building. 3 As a whole Mesa Wind Veils are 50% open, reducing cooling requirements by as much as 30% at some times of the year.

3

Impression of Rain //
Vogt Landschaftsarchitekten + Meili, Peter Architekten

Weather Garden, The Park Hyatt Hotel, Zurich, Switzerland

In this evocative interpretation of a stone garden, weather leaves its traces within patterns of rain puddles. As a courtyard within the Park Hyatt Hotel, set against the backdrop of Zurich's sky, the space is designed for viewing from the surrounding hotel rooms. The design emphasizes a temporal experience, where small reflecting pools of rainwater mirror the changing sky as they evaporate.

Within the garden, a single stone platform acts as a stage for this fleeting weather performance. It consists of rectangular stone slabs that were cut and ground to have various concave and convex profiles. When it rains, the undulated surface forms a landscape of puddles. Since each puddle differs in size and depth the evaporation rates vary, producing a sequence morphing of shapes.

This evaporating installation visualizes the elusive hydrological cycle. ALTHOUGH A SUBTLE INTERVENTION, THE STONE STAGE HIGHLIGHTS THE MATERIALITY OF RAINWATER AND ITS PHASE-CHANGING QUALI-TIES. It poetically frames the common and often overlooked streetscape following rain. It also makes a simple connection between the vanishing puddles to the clouds drifting above as their origin and destination.

1 A simple stone platform acts as a stage for a fleeting weather performance. **2** The stone slabs are polished to have alternating concave and convex profiles. **3** The rain evaporates at varying rates depending on the profiles of the stones. **4** The rain puddles mirror the changing sky as they evaporate.

1

2

3

4

G-Sky Green Wall Panels

G-Sky Green Wall Panels are a patented modular planting system for 90° angled walls. They are suitable for interior and exterior wall applications and can thrive in a variety of environmental conditions. The 1x1ft (0.3 x 0.3m) panels can be arranged as needed to create a living cladding for a wall. The arrangement and selection of plants can also be customized to suit local conditions and design requirements.

The modular panels are made of an ultraviolet-resistant, non-flammable Polypropylene. Each panel contains a growing medium of natural peat block, encased in a non-woven, non-corrosive, non-flammable fabric. The panels are ~3in (82 – 89mm) deep and are mounted on a stainless steel or aluminum frame that is anchored into a concrete wall of other adequate structure.

The panels are shipped with 13 or 25 established plants growing out of the large perforations in the fabric. Plant species are selected for their ability to grow in 90° orientation and within the environmental conditions of the installed wall. Water is supplied to the plants with the G-Sky GWP Drip Irrigation System with pressure-compensating emitters. Depending on the selection, plants generally grow approximately 3 to 8in (76 – 200mm) from the panels to form a dense carpet of living green material.

Anticipated maintenance for the system is low. Weeding and some plant replacement are expected. Pruning and liquid fertilizer application, injected via the drip system, are recommended to keep the plants healthy over the long term.

Manufacturer: G-SKY, Inc.

Earth Cinch

Launch	Stratify	Fluid	Grooming	Digestive	Translate	Volatile

Earth Cinch is proposed as a transitional biodegradable growth system for vertical or horizontal vegetated surfaces. Using Ingeo™ fibers, made of NatureWorks™ PLA (Poly Lactic Acid), a biopolymer produced by Dow Cargill, Earth Cinch features a quilted construction with a series of soil and seed-filled pockets. The pockets are stitched to create an undulating planting surface. Over time, the material will biodegrade, leaving no material or product residue.

Envisioned as a temporary vegetative cover for abandoned urban sites, such as parking lots or derelict building façades, Earth Cinch was primarily developed as a thickened earth tapestry that could be easily deployed without the labor of planting, or the expense and construction of plant containers. It can be manufactured as a mass-produced product. Upon installation over a wall, a contaminated ground or a rooftop, the embedded seeds sprout and transform urban blight into a growing medium.

The porosity of the fabric allows for rainwater irrigation, air circulation and drainage. The Ingeo™ fibers' hydrophilic properties allow it to have high water absorption. In combination with its quilted structure, the fabric absorbs and retains water temporarily and conducts water across the surface to the plants. In addition to having a high dimensional stability, resilience and ultraviolet resistance, the Ingeo™ fabric also provides a delicate shimmer that exceeds the visual quality of traditional industrial geotextiles.

Design: Freecell

Flexterra® & Soil Guard

Launch	Stratify	Fluid	Grooming	Digestive	Translate	Volatile

Flexible Growth Medium (FGM) & Bonded Fiber Matrix (BFM) are two types of hydraulically applied erosion control materials, designed as transitional soil stabilization systems. Composed of loose natural fibers and a binder, the matrix biodegrades within a year, as newly planted vegetation establishes roots, and provides long-term erosion protection. The hydraulic application allows the fiber mix to be sprayed from a distance onto inaccessible or dangerously steep areas, with slope ratios ranging from up to 1:1, as well as onto irregular surfaces. Typical applications include residential lawns, golf courses, earthwork, highway projects, stream channel stabilization, and mine reclamation.

FGM Flexterra® is made of thermally processed long-strand wood fibers (Poplar, Pine and Oak), a co-polymer gel, and a vegetable hydro-colloid tackifier. Within two hours post application, the fibers bond internally and to the soil, gaining a blanket-like consistency, creating an instant effective erosion-resistant blanket. BFM Soil Guard is made of thermally treated and mechanically de-fibrated wood fiber (Aspen/Birch), a polysaccharide guar binder, and a slow release fertilizer. Both the FGM and BFM may be applied onto a newly seeded ground or combined with seeds to achieve a one-step application.

The mix disperses rapidly in water and remains in uniform suspension under agitation, forming homogenous slurry for spray application. Once applied, the fibers form a continuous and strong moisture-retaining mat that conforms to the terrain contours. The water-resistant matrix requires no curing time, and is therefore effective as a rapid slope stabilization system for installations just prior to heavy rains.

In comparison to Erosion Control Blankets (ECB), FGM and BFM do not have as high a tensile or shear strength, but they offer higher soil coverage and reduced soil loss from slopes during rain events. In addition, FGM and BFM do not require site preparation, reducing installation costs in comparison to ECB, which require extensive grading and staking. FGM and BFM can be used in conjunction with erosion control nettings in installations requiring a higher tensile strength, such as stream banks and shorelines, where sites are exposed to high-velocity wind or water.

Manufacturer: Profile Products LLC; Mat, Inc.

SaiCoir Erosion Net, BioNet, Nedia Erosion Control Blankets

Launch	Stratify	Fluid	Grooming	Digestive	Translate	Volatile

Biodegradable erosion control geotextiles are made of natural fibers and designed as transitional soil stabilization systems. The geotextiles protect exposed slopes from erosion and slowly biodegrade. The textiles are typically made of straw, coir (coconut husk) or jute (*Corchorus tiliaceae*) fibers, and manufactured in large rolls of woven, knit, and non-woven textiles, with some varieties containing embedded seed mixes. The textiles are anchored or staked to the surface of slopes, stream banks, and shorelines. Often stitched with biodegradable jute or coir nettings, photodegradable or ultraviolet stabilized polypropylene nettings, each textile product varies in longevity (from three months to eight years), flow velocity capacity (8 – 16ft/sec, 2.4 – 4.9m/sec), and slope ratio applicability (from 4:1 to 1:1).

Standard geotextile rolls measure 4ft – 13ft (1.2 – 3.9m) wide and up to 225ft (68.5m) long. Coir fibers are also made into the cylindrical form of logs to provide a stable growing medium along shorelines, stream banks and wetlands. The logs are stacked into the ground and planted with wetland plant varieties. The logs resist and buffer erosion from flowing water while trapping silt and sediment, creating a protected, aerated and hydrated growing zone for plants. Comparatively, erosion control blankets have a higher longevity, tensile and shear strength than hydraulically applied products (i.e. bonded fiber matrix). They may be more appropriate for steep slope gradients, or in extreme weather conditions with high flow velocities. However, the textiles do not provide full soil coverage and are more labor-intensive to install.

The textiles are fungi- and ultraviolet-resistant. While porous, they have high water-holding capacity and can absorb up to five times their weight in water, releasing moisture slowly back into the ground, and thus enhancing seed germination and early plant growth. The textiles have an ideal pH for plant growth and high cation exchange capacity. In addition, they inhibit root pathogens such as *Pithium* and *Phtothora*, while promoting strong root systems. Common applications include retention ponds and wetland construction, riparian area protection, drainage ditches and intermittent flow channels, dams, lake and waterway shore preservation, hydro-seeding and high-altitude plantings, mining reclamation, landfill rehabilitation, highway and rail embankments, eroded seashore and dune stabilization areas, and ski slopes.

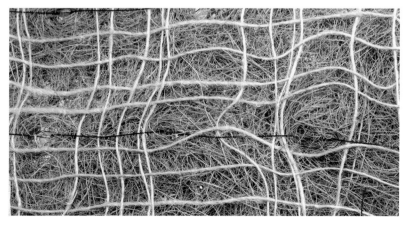

Manufacturers: Sai International Trading Corporation; North America Green; Nedia Enterprises, Inc.

Envirogrid

Launch	Stratify	Fluid	Grooming	Digestive	Translate	Volatile

Envirogrid is a flexible and expandable cellular soil confinement structure that combines compaction resistance with drainage to provide slope and stream bank erosion control, as well as ground and retaining wall stabilization. Originally developed by the Corps of Engineers, the confinement structure is generically known as geocell. The cells are made of strips of thermo-welded High Density Polyethylene (HDPE) that when expanded can be filled with vegetation, aggregate, concrete or combinations thereof. Each geocell mat is made of 58 strips of solid or perforated HDPE in a section length of 29 cells and 5 cells wide; 142in (3.6m) in length with heights ranging from 2 – 8in (5.1cm – 20.4cm).

Envirogrid is an alternative for geotextiles, hydroseeding, gabion baskets, and concrete reinforcement for slope stabilization. For example, it offers an economy of aggregate quantities in comparison with geotextile-aggregate layer construction. Its expanded cell walls keep the aggregate from being pushed away from the applied load, while applied loads are spread over an extended surface area.

While hydroseeding can be employed to hold soil and seed in place until vegetation gets established, this technique may not be adequate to control erosion caused by high water velocities associated with steep slopes. Envirogrid reinforces root systems and directs hydraulic flows over the top of cells, with the cells acting as a series of check dams, thereby preventing formation of rills and gullies. It controls the migration of fills by hydraulic and gravitational forces, through the dissipation of hydraulic energy in and underneath cells and by confinement of fill material within cells. In addition, water is trapped in the cells and percolates to the soil.

A geocell section filled with local soils can be an economical solution to both cut and fill situations. In very steep slope applications soils can be retained with a geocell vertical wall structure. The cells not only hold the soil in place, they also provide drainage throughout the structure. Its large surface area allows for great compaction resistance and for the support of heavy loads such as trucks.

The flexible nature of the concrete-filled cellular confinement system permits conformance with subgrade movement without the potential cracking and undermining associated with poured-in-place concrete slabs. Installation costs are dramatically reduced through elimination of costly forms and other construction techniques typically related to concrete channel lining. In areas with limited easements, stacked cellular confinement-wall slopes along channels allow the use of vegetative, granular or concrete fills in the outer cells in order to steepen slopes and to increase resistance to higher flow rates.

Manufacturer: GeoProducts

Land.Tiles

| Launch | Stratify | Fluid | Grooming | Digestive | Translate | Volatile |

Land.Tiles is an exploration of a modular erosion control system that conforms to site-specific terrain and dynamic flows. Generated within the context of prosaic erosion control and slope stabilization systems, Land. Tiles attempts an alternative model. The design of the modular components and their configuration are thought of as an integral part of the architectural design process, creating performance and programmatic gradients between areas of soil retention, erosion control, walking surfaces, permeable and vegetated areas, and irrigation control areas.

As part of the exploration, a temporary installation tested the potential of integrated topographical and flow analysis with site-specific installation of the various tile permutation. 140 concrete cast and textured blocks were manufactured through a digital design and fabrication process of CNC milling and vacuum-formed plastic. Every tile features similar sectional characteristics derived from a textile process of "double pleating" producing the articulation of a single continuous surface by means of local inflections. Through a process of subdivision, every tile adjusts to its site-specific condition and programmatic designation, while maintaining its prototypic geometry. The modules range in textures, morphology and shape to accommodate a variability of water flow through attenuation, retention, infiltration to the soil, as well as redirection for irrigation.

Design: PATTERNS / Marcelo Spina

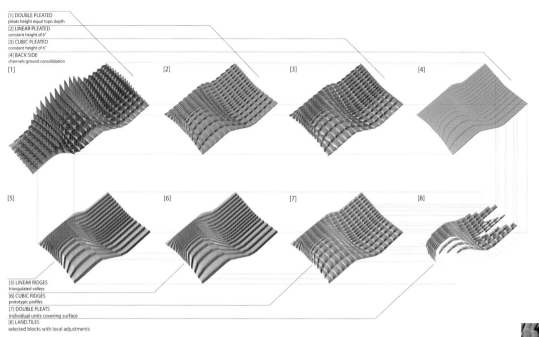

[1] DOUBLE PLEATED
pleats height equal topo depth

[2] LINEAR PLEATED
constant height of 6"

[3] CUBIC PLEATED
constant height of 6"

[4] BACK SIDE
channels ground consolidation

[1] [2] [3] [4]

[5] [6] [7] [8]

[5] LINEAR RIDGES
triangulated valleys

[6] CUBIC RIDGES
prototypic profiles

[7] DOUBLE PLEATS
individual units covering surface

[8] LAND.TILES
selected blocks with local adjustments

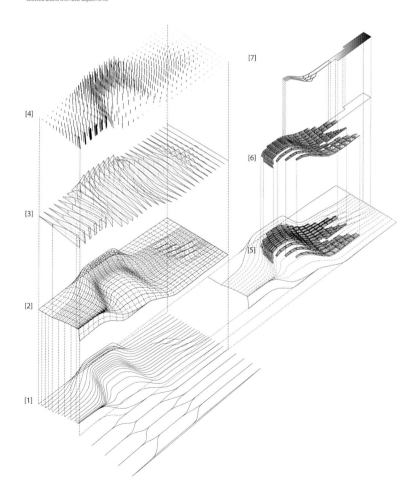

[7]

[4]

[6]

[3]

[5]

[2]

[1]

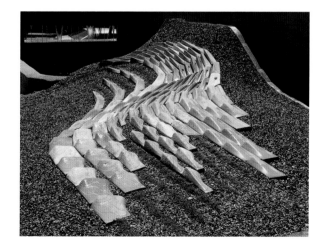

Cornell University (CU)-Structural Soil™ and Amsterdam Tree Sand

Launch	Stratify	Fluid	Grooming	Digestive	Translate	Volatile

A major impediment to the success of tree growth in urban conditions is the lack of soil volume. Without sufficient soil volume to expand their root systems, the plants and trees are impacted in a number of ways, including their total growth, susceptibility to disease and drought, and long-term survival. Structural soils address this problem by creating an engineered medium that can both meet load-bearing requirements and serve as a medium for root growth. They use a combination of organic material and structural materials to create a medium that can be used as a subgrade underneath paved surfaces or surface for traffic and still maintain sufficient aeration, drainage, and flexibility for root growth. By allowing the growth of roots underneath paved surfaces, structural soils allow for a greater integration of trees in constructed environments, and reduce the likelihood of sidewalks heaving from restricted root growth. There are two types of structural soils: Cornell University Structural Soil™ and Amsterdam Tree Sand.

Cornell University Structural Soil (U.S. Patent # 5,849,069) employs a lattice of crushed stone as the structural basis of the medium. The soil is "gap-graded" such that intermediately-sized soil particles are excluded, preventing them from filling in the space within the lattice that enables proper aeration and drainage. Heavy clay loam and organic matter are mixed with the crushed stones to provide water, nutrient-holding, and cation exchange capacity. The complete soil recipe calls for crushed stone (granite or limestone) graded from ¾ – 1½in (1.3 – 1.9cm), clay loam conforming to USDA soil classification system with < 30% gravel, 25 – 30% sand, 20 – 40% silt, 25 – 40% clay, and a small amount of Gelscape® hydrogel stabilizing agent, which acts as a tackifier.

Heicom's Amsterdam Tree Sand was developed in Holland and is now manufactured world-wide under the brand name Amsterdam Tree Sand or Soil. With over 20 years of application, it has proven to be an effective medium for urban trees. It generally consists of 60 – 70% graded silica sand and 30 – 40% organic matter produced from composting landscape trimmings. The quality of silica granules allows the soil to achieve 85% – 90% compaction, thus supporting paving and resisting compaction from pedestrian and vehicular traffic. The silica's texture also allows for oxygen and moisture to reach the root zone and support healthy tree growth. Added organic matter increases the soil's aeration, water retention, and available nutrients.

Sources: Urban Horticulture Institute, Department of Horticulture, Cornell University; Heicom, UK

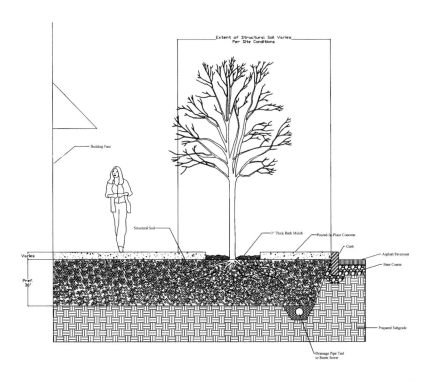

EnduraSafe™

| Launch | **Stratify** | **Fluid** | **Grooming** | Digestive | Translate | Volatile |

EnduraSafe™ is a recycled rubber product that is typically used as an alternative to natural-based mulches in landscaping application, and as a resilient surfacing material for shock-absorption applications in playgrounds and outdoor sports facilities. Made from discarded automobile and truck tires, the thermoset polymer rubber cannot be re-melted and is therefore chopped into aggregate particles (i.e. mulch), and bound by a polymeric binder for poured-in-place applications of seamless surface.

In contrast to wood mulch, the rubber material does not wick any moisture from the soil under dry conditions and helps retain moisture content in the soil, thus reducing irrigation needs. It is denser than wood mulch and will not blow in the wind or float away during a rainstorm. Thus while not biodegradable, it does not require annual replacement or replenishment. The rubber is mold-, fungus-, and insect-resistant. Typically installed at a 1.5in (3.8cm) depth for general landscaping applications, the rubber has high compression resistance. It has colorfastness to ultraviolet exposure guaranteed to be fade-resistant for 8–10 years. Nine standard rubber mulch colors include: brown, copper, cypress, grass green, redwood, black, bouncing blue, laughing lilac, and tumbling turquoise. Custom colors are available as well.

As a safety product for playground application, the rubber mulch is installed at a 4–6in (10.2–15.2cm) depth to protect from falls ranging 7–13ft (2.1–3.9m). Installation depths are determined based on the Critical Fall Height standards, defined as the relation between fall-height from play equipment to severe injury, in order to determine the level of resilience needed to absorb the shock of the fall.

EnduraSafe™ is wheelchair accessible per ADA (Americans with Disabilities Act) specifications (ASTM F1951–99) and is shock absorbing under ASTM (American Society for Testing and Materials) F1292.

Manufacturer: Advanced Ground Care Products LLC

Porous Concrete & Asphalt

Launch	Stratify	Fluid	Grooming	Digestive	Translate	Volatile

Asphalt and concrete can be mixed in a manner that creates a series of voids that allow water and air to travel through. Such porous pavements are effective at mitigating stormwater runoff. While porous asphalt is more economical than porous concrete, both materials have been successfully employed in the field with installations over 20 years old. Both are conventional mixtures, from which fine particles have been graded from the aggregate mix. The void content left by this gap-grading is approximately 15 – 25%, sufficient space for rapid infiltration during most rain events. Clogging of these voids can be avoided with proper grading to prevent sources of silt from reaching the pavement unfiltered. Also street cleaners are recommended to clean the porous surfaces twice a year or when surfaces have been clogged.

A stone bed, usually 18 – 36in (45.1 – 91.4cm) deep, lies underneath the porous materials and retains stormwater until it infiltrates into the soil mantle. The stone bed can be enlarged to also accept stormwater from additional sources, such as roofs and adjacent impervious paved areas. In some situations, such as areas with poor water infiltration, parts of the infiltration bed may be situated away from the porous paving, where infiltration is improved or amended, and connected with drains. The extra thick subgrade layer also serves as an enhanced foundation for the paving. The long-term endurance of some early installations of porous materials is in part attributed to its enhanced foundation. Additionally, the combination of the improved insulation provided by the extra subgrade and the porosity of the paving materials acts to melt snows faster than impervious paving, thus reducing the need for plowing and salting snow.

Though porous pavement is used primarily for parking areas, it is suitable for a wide range of applications, including paths and sports areas. The absence of fine particles creates a surface that is generally rougher than regular paving. Structurally, the absence of fine particles does reduce the shear strength capability of the material and it is not recommended for sloped surfaces. Material additives such as lava rock can adjust the performance of the pavement, including increasing the shear strength and water retention capacity. Porous pavements are comparable in cost to regular pavement materials, however the extra subgrade will incur extra costs. These costs may be easily offset by the drainage infrastructure required for typical installations.

Source: Portland Cement Association; National Ready Mixed Concrete Association; Cahill Associates

Soil Cement

| Launch | Stratify | Fluid | Grooming | Digestive | Translate | Volatile |

Soil cement is a highly compacted mixture of soil, or other salvaged aggregate, Portland cement, and water. Soil cement and Portland cement differ in several ways, including their general physical compositions and appropriate uses. It is cost effective, since as much as 90% of its materials are obtained on-site. Existing soil, deteriorated roads, cinders, foundry sands, and screening from quarries and gravel pits can all be utilized as mixing materials. Virtually any inorganic soil can be used, though granular soils are favored over clay soils. Using site soils in the soil cement can improve the visual and physical connection between the existing landscape and the new intervention.

In general, soil cement has good compressive and shear strength, but low tensile strength and some brittleness, making it prone to forming cracks. Because soil cement forms a very rigid material with slab-like characteristics, the required thicknesses for roads and other surfaces are less than those required for granular bases. It can also be designed to be virtually impermeable, making it particularly resistant to freeze-thaw and suitable for high-intensity hydrological uses. Simple laboratory tests establish the cement content, compaction, and water characteristics required to achieve structural performance. Specimens taken from roads show that the strength of soil cement actually increases with age; some specimens from roads were four times as strong following four years of traffic.

Mixing soil cement with on-site materials is a simple multi-step process. The proper amount of cement is spread over the existing soil, then the cement, soil, and water are mixed by any of several types of mixing machines. Next, the mixture is heavily compacted with common machines to obtain the maximum benefits associated with the material. Finally, it is cured. When off-site materials are used the soil cement can be mixed off-site in a concrete plant and hauled to site and spread, compacted, and cured.

Soil cement is commonly used in a wide range of applications. In addition to serving as a general-purpose paving surface, it is often used for stream bank protection, channel liners, drop structures, pond liners, and retaining walls. Its impermeability, stiffness, and economical characteristics have made it an ideal material for large-scale hydrological infrastructure projects. The material's more naturalistic finish is ideal for blending hydrological reinforcements into the existing landscape. Soil cement can also be mixed directly in the ground with lower concentrations of Portland cement to create a material akin to soft rock; these ground modification techniques are useful for foundations, retaining structures, or temporary support.

Source: Portland Cement Association

Soil Moist, Stockabsorb®, Watersorb®, PetroGuard, Oasis

Launch	Stratify	Fluid	Grooming	Digestive	Translate	Volatile

Super-absorbent polymers (SAP) are engineered to retain 200–400 times their own weight in water or other liquid. Once submerged in water the SAP absorb water at an extremely rapid rate and swell into a gel. It is through osmotic pressure that the SAP absorb and release the liquid, and thus, unlike a sponge, the gel will not leach when applied with pressure. Manufactured into multiple forms such as granules, fibers, nonwoven, knitted and woven textiles, SAP have a wide range of applications from personal hygiene products (i.e. pads, diapers) and medical surgery spill-control, to irrigation control for horticulture and agriculture, wire and cable water blocking, and toxic spill cleanup.

Within the landscape and horticultural field, SAP are generically known as Hydrogel and commercially known, among many other brand names, as Soil Moist, Stockabsorb®, Oasis Super Absorbent Fiber, PetroGuard, Watersorb®. Made of polyacrylate/polyacrylamide copolymers, the SAP were originally designed for use in conditions where there is high electrolyte or mineral content and a need for long term stability including numerous wet/dry cycles, such as in agriculture and horticulture. The driving force for the osmotic pressure is typically the higher concentration of sodium or potassium ions in the polymer than in its surrounding environment. Thus, water is drawn in and out of the polymer in an attempt to reach equilibrium. For landscape and agricultural uses, the exceptional absorption capacity is utilized to increase the soil's water-holding capacity by 50–100%, thus reducing irrigation requirements, fertilizer washout, stormwater runoff and soil erosion. Conversely, when the soil is dry and plants are in need of water, the SAP control-release the retained water and fertilizer to the growing plants through osmotic pressure. The SAP improve aeration in soil, reduce transplant shock, and prevent soil compaction, thus encouraging deep root penetration.

SAP granules can be integrated into soil mixes, or used as tackifiers in hydroseeding applications. Woven or nonwoven geotextiles are used for land water management and control, and can potentially be used for flood protection due to their extremely rapid rates of absorption. Engineered to have various filtering and absorption properties, SAP can be hydrophobic and demonstrate high capacity to absorb reactive chemicals, aliphatic and aromatic hydrocarbons and chlorocarbons, making them ideal for containing and removing chemical spills.

Manufacturers: JRM Chemical, Inc.; Stockhausen, Inc.; Polymers, Inc.; Advanced Polymeric Absorbents; Technical Absorbents Limited

Bridgestone Rubber Dam

Launch	Stratify	Fluid	Grooming	Digestive	Translate	Volatile

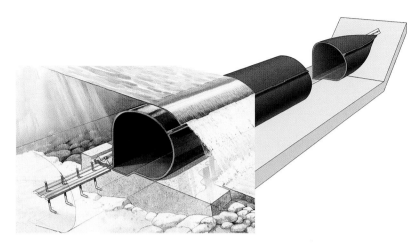

Inflatable dams are becoming increasingly popular within waterways, due to their ability to deflate easily and quickly in order to prevent upstream flooding. The technology has been available for 30 years and more than 2,200 inflatable dams are in use around the world. The dams are best suited for small to medium-sized watercourses, where width is much greater than height. Compared to other adjustable dams, they allow for long spans with few structural piers, which ultimately reduces floodwater interference when the dam is deflated. Given the potentially temporary status of the dams they are suitable for a wide range of purposes, including hydroelectricity, groundwater recharge, water supply, flood control, irrigation, water treatment, tidal barriers and recreation.

The Bridgestone rubber dams are made of heavy-duty Nylon-reinforced rubber, with an EPDM (Ethylene Propylene Diene Monomer) cover to withstand ultraviolet light. Each section of the rubber is embedded with a fabric mesh and ceramic chips to resist tearing. The rubber also contains a self-sealing material for small holes. Once inflated, the dams can reach up to 20ft (6m) tall with spans over 60ft (18.2m). The thickness of bladder ranges from 9.5 – 25mm (0.4 – 1in), depending upon the dam height.

Each bladder has a thin fin on top, which spreads water flow evenly over the surface of the dam to prevent swaying of the bladder and possible tears. The fin structure also facilitates the flattening of the bladder during flood events. In some cases it is possible for people to enter into the bladder through an airtight chamber. Inflation and deflation can be manually or automatically controlled. With an upstream monitoring system detecting varying water levels, the automatic control system adjusts the air pressure in the dam to maintain the desired water level.

The dams are anchored to a foundation using a simple clamping system composed of anchor bolts and steel clamping plates. Unlike steel gates, they can be installed in rivers with any side-slope angle, eliminating the necessity of adjusting the riverbank. Air is supplied using a low-pressure blower system. Because of the relatively few moving parts, inflatable dams are highly reliable and require little maintenance.

Manufacturer: Bridgestone Industrial Products America, Inc.

Biobarrier®

Biobarrier® is a non-woven geotextile engineered to control root growth in order to prevent encroachment toward structures. Biobarrier® consists of composite nodules injection-molded through Typar®, a spunbonded polypropylene fabric. The permanently attached nodules release a growth-control herbicide called trifluralin, which adsorbs in the soil. The patented slow-release process delivers a precise amount of trifluralin necessary to inhibit root growth.

Once released, the trifluralin degrades but is continuously replaced by new material, building and maintaining a root inhibition zone. Spaced 1.5in (3.8cm) apart the individual nodule zones overlap, creating a contiguous growth inhibition area. When roots enter the inhibition zone, root tip cells cannot divide, preventing growth in that direction. Trifluralin is not systemic; therefore, it is not taken into the plant. As a result, the root system is diverted away from the Biobarrier® protected structure without adversely affecting the desirable plants or trees. Root branches outside of the zone are not affected.

Trifluralin has been used over 40 years to prevent weed growth in agricultural application. It is nontoxic and has an EPA toxicity rating of class IV, making it, as manufacturer Reemay states, "slightly more toxic than sugar but less than salt". Due to extremely low water solubility, it does not leach. And with high soil adsorption, it does not tend to migrate. In addition, the released chemical decomposes within a period of six months or less, and does not persist in the ground.

Biobarrier® fabric is placed between the root source and the structure. Typical applications include landscape beds, nursery potting, underground septic tanks and sewer lines, building foundations, electrical tower, and hazardous waste caps. It can also be used to prevent root intrusion into earth-filled structures and drain systems associated with dams, dikes and canals. The textile's flexibility allows for custom installation. Its porosity allows for air, nutrients and water exchange in the soil.

Ranging in dimensions from 12in x 20ft to 58.5in x 100ft (30.5cm x 6m to 148.6cm x 30.5m) Biobarrier® can be installed in the soil vertically, horizontally or wrapped around various structures. Pegs are often necessary to suspend or secure the textile in place. Fabric should extend a minimum of 18in (45.7cm) beyond the structure area to be protected as roots can grow around the edges of fabric. For vertical applications, the top edge must be even with the soil surface. A minimum of 2in (5cm) soil overlay should also be maintained for horizontal applications. Retrofit applications where roots are already present require root pruning.

Manufacturer: BBA Nonwovens: Reemay, Inc.

Controlled Burning

Launch	Stratify	Fluid	Grooming	Digestive	Translate	Volatile

Prescribed or controlled burning is a technique conventionally used in forest management, farming, and prairie restoration to control violent fires, and to maintain and renew targeted ecosystems. While controlled burning is primarily employed to reduce the hazard of violent or extended wildfires by consuming the combustible layer, it has many additional benefits. These include improving wildlife habitats, controlling competing vegetation, improving forage for grazing, improving visual appeal and accessibility, controlling plant diseases, and perpetuating fire-dependent species.

The timing of the prescribed burn determines the survival of desired plants and the impact on wildlife species. Burning to favor desired grasses takes place just as the grasses start to green and the soil surface is damp. Generally, a late spring burn controls woody vegetation and cool-season grasses better than an early spring burn; however, it does not benefit the growth of wildflowers. This burning time provides warm-season grasses with the nutrients they need to grow. Before burning, nesting times of grassland species should be considered to prevent the destruction of nests. Though fall burns are possible and can be beneficial, they are often avoided, due to cooler temperatures, drier ground and destruction to winter wildlife habitats.

There are four basic burn techniques used in the prescribed burning of grasslands. These techniques include a backfire, a parallel or flank fire, a perimeter fire and a strip head fire. Each method has strengths and weaknesses, depending on the weather conditions, size of the area and available expertise. A backfire is used downwind of the burn site and is considered the coolest and safest fire; however, it is slower burning and therefore takes longer. The fire is ignited on the downwind side of the fuel and slowly burns into the field against the wind, expanding the firebreak. A parallel or flank fire burns hotter and faster than a backfire and works well on square or circular parcels. A fire is ignited on the sides of the burn site parallel to the wind direction at the same time or soon after a backfire is lit. A perimeter fire is not only one of the quickest burn methods, but it also creates a much hotter fire, which can be harder to control. This method starts with a backfire, followed by lighting the flanks, and finishes by lighting the upwind side of the burn site, called the head of the site. This head fire moves rapidly towards the flanks and backfire. A strip head fire burns slightly faster than a backfire and is relatively safe and works well for burning rectangular or odd-shaped parcels. It is also cost-effective in comparison to other burns. A series of strips are lit, starting at the downwind side of the site, burning only one at a time. This is ideal when burning with only a limited number of personnel.

Sources: Ministry of Forests and Range; U.S. Environmental Protection Agency

Toxic Filtration via Fungi

Launch	Stratify	Fluid	Grooming	**Digestive**	Translate	Volatile

Mycofiltration is a term coined by mycologist Paul Stamets that refers to the use of mycelium mats as biological filters for the purpose of toxic soil remediation. Mycelium is the vegetative part of a fungus consisting of a vast network of fine filaments that exists below the ground, permeating the soil. It is a saprophyte that works symbiotically with nearly all plants, by breaking down biomass and chemical compounds into their basic constituents, providing nutrients for plant uptake.

Together with Battelle Laboratories, a non-profit foundation in the bioremediation industry, Stamets has been developing a patent for the utilization of mycelia to decompose toxic waste, a process termed Mycoremediation. The research work is based on the fact that mycelium produces enzymes and acids that break down woody plants into lignin and cellulose, and decompose hydrocarbons, the base structure present in oils, petroleum products, pesticides, PCBs (Polychlorinated biphenyls), and many other pollutants.

Stamets-Battelle studies have shown that oyster mushrooms can break down heavy oil, consisting of polycyclic aromatic hydrocarbons, into non-toxic components. Other strains of fungi can fully consume *E. coli* bacteria. The Stamets-Battelle research also showed that as the mushrooms rot, a sequence of other biological processes ensues. Flies populate the area, consuming the fungus; those attract other insects, which in turn bring in birds; the birds disperse seeds, enhancing plant cultivation and diversity.

The growth momentum of mycelia is tremendous. Mycelial mass can grow outwards at a rate of ¼ – 2in/day (1– 5cm), with some individual fungus covering more than 20,000ac (8,094ha). Rapid site coverage is highly efficient for soil remediation. The Stamets-Battelle team poses buffer zones around streams as ideal sites for Mycoremediation. Around stream buffers, debris from trees and shrubs, combined with grasses provide a rich biomass supply, while mycelia filters out runoff from adjacent farms, highways and suburban zones.

Research: Paul Stamets, Fungi Perfecti + Battelle Laboratories

Land Imprinting

Launch	Stratify	Fluid	Grooming	Digestive	Translate	Volatile

Imprinting is a simple technique for re-vegetating land that has undergone de-sertification or degradation. The process imitates the effect of natural impressions left by hoofed herd animals. The troughs left by the imprinting machine concentrate water and nutrients to help germinate and support seedlings. The technique is particularly suited for the establishment of perennial plants, which require greater moisture to germinate, and in arid climates where moisture is generally too scarce for unassisted seed germination.

The process begins with a tractor-pulled imprinting roller that creates 10in (25cm) V-shaped troughs in the soil. A seeder, driven from the imprinting roller, delivers seeds to the imprinted surfaces. Each imprinted trough or "micro-watershed" can hold several liters of rainwater, enough to establish one or more seedlings. 2in (5cm) dikes separate the staggered troughs and help hold rainwater until it infiltrates the soil. Following imprinting, infiltration rates within the first hour of a rainfall event increase by a factor of ten or more. The deep moisture infiltration in the soil favors the establishment of perennial vegetation over less desirable annuals. The troughs also provide a microclimatic increase in humidity and can shield the young seedlings from excessive sunlight and dry winds. With proper soil condition, imprints are stable enough to wait several years for sufficient rain to foster seed germination.

Imprinting technique supercedes any prior preparation to the existing soils. Tilling is not recommended as this may destroy existing vegetation, cover plant litter, disturb soil structure and encourage weed growth. While imprinting may cut down plants, it does not dislodge their roots and re-growth from their crown is likely. In hard soil conditions the imprinter can be adjusted to apply greater pressure or simply applied multiple times. Additionally, mycorrhizal inoculum can be injected into the soil during the process to help plant establishment in harsh conditions.

Manufacturer: Western Ecology, LLC

Naturaire® Systems

Launch	Stratify	Fluid	Grooming	Digestive	Translate	Volatile

The Naturaire® Indoor Air Biofilter is an interior plantscape – a vertical hydroponic green wall that contains a range of foliage and flowering plants capable of removing common indoor contaminants. The technology is based on biofiltration, a technology commonly found in industrial application to remediate waste air streams. Air is passed over a biologically active media (beneficial microbes) to break down the contaminants.

The plants are selected according to their ability to facilitate biofiltration, grow in the hydroponic media, and withstand indoor conditions with varying levels of light and temperature. Although a range of plants can be used, woody tropical species such as *Ficus spp.* and *Schefflera spp.* have been found to be very effective.

The construction of the green wall includes a 2in (5cm) thick synthetic mat, into which plants are rooted. Water is circulated from a reservoir in the base and pumped to the top of the wall where it trickles out to irrigate the plants. Air is actively drawn through the biofilter via a fan system that is installed in the back of the green wall. As the air passes through the irrigated plants, it is cooled, so that when distributed through the building's HVAC system it contributes to temperature regulation and conservation of cooling energy.

The Naturaire® Biofilter is robust and can be adapted to a wide range of retrofits or new building venues. It can improve the indoor environment by reducing contaminant levels, and by regulating temperature and humidity. Tested under laboratory conditions, up to 90% of the formaldehyde was removed with a single pass of the indoor air biofilter. Microbial action around the root zone degrades pollutants such as formaldehyde and benzene into their benign constituents such as water and carbon dioxide.

Manufacturer: Air Quality Solutions Ltd

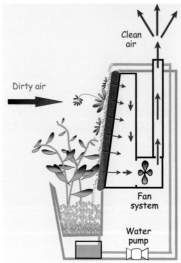

TXActive® – Photocatalytic Cement

| Launch | Stratify | Fluid | Grooming | Digestive | Translate | Volatile |

TXActive® is a photocatalytic cement that can reduce organic and inorganic pollutants in the air. Photocatalysis is a natural phenomenon, in which a substance, termed the photocatalyzer, alters the speed of a chemical reaction through the action of light. By exploiting the energy of light, photocatalyzers induce the formation of strongly oxidizing agents, which can cause the decomposition of some organic and inorganic substances present in the atmosphere.

Upon contact with the surface of the TXActive®, airborne pollutants emitted by car exhaust and heating systems consisting of Nitric oxides (NOx), sulfur dioxides, and carbon monoxide get converted into innocuous salts. A mere 3min exposure to the sun is sufficient to obtain a reduction in polluting agents of up to 75%. In a large city such as Milan, researchers have calculated that covering 15% of visible urban surfaces with products containing TXActive® would enable a reduction in pollution of approximately 50%.

A first test on a photocatalytic TXActive® mortar was used to cover the asphalt surface of a section of Via Morandi in Segrate (province of Milan); a road that is 230m (766ft) long and 10m (30ft) wide, and which every day sees traffic flow of around 1,000 vehicles/hour. Monitoring proved a reduction in nitric oxides on the road of around 60%.

Other products on the market that use Italcementi's photocatalytics technology are mortar, paint, and paving. In Japan, the technology has been used to make self-cleaning lamps, car coatings and construction materials, fog-resistant mirrors and glass, antibacterial tiles and fibers, and air purifiers.

Manufacturer: Essroc, Italcementi Group

BioHaven™ Wild Floating Islands

BioHaven™ Wild Floating Islands are a floating habitat, effective in maintaining the health of waterways due to a combination of specially selected plants, high surface area substrate, and a proprietary microbe and aeration system. They may be applied to a eutrophic water body, water garden, stream, river, or wastewater application, in order to remove excess nutrients, heavy metals, or hazardous substances.

The microbes work with the substrate and plant roots to remove excess nutrients from the water, thereby greatly reducing algae growth and eutrophication. Fish benefit from improved water quality, as roots underwater provide a food source and habitat. The islands also provide shelter, nesting, spawning, feeding and resting habitat for a diverse population of birds, frogs, lizards, turtles, and aquatic invertebrates species.

While plants feed off the nutrients in the water, the microbes dismantle the nutrient and convert them into forms usable by plants. Since the microbes work faster than algae to process nutrients, the algae consequently starve. The water is oxygenated so that the fish, frogs, and aquatic invertebrates can breathe. In addition, the generation of gases surrounding plant roots contributes to the buoyancy of the island.

The plant substrate is a recycled polymer matrix bonded with marine foam, which allows water circulation and plant growth through the substrate. Compared to earthen islands, the BioHaven™ Wild Floating Islands are lighter, easier and less expensive to install, allowing plants to establish faster.

The substrate and wetland plant root hair provide multiple surface area attachment points for colonization of specific nitrogen- and phosphorus-reducing microbes. Microbes convert ammonia nitrogen ($NH_3 - N$) to Nitrate NO_3. Specific bacteria can be injected into the floating islands at installation and also periodically to maintain efficiency of the biofiltration process. Specific surface areas of the bio-filters can be adjusted according to the level of pollutants.

BioHavens™ can be made in any size, and can be customized to achieve higher levels of buoyancy. A 500sf (46.5m²) BioHaven™ can support up to 1000lbs (453.5kg) of weight, to include people, walkways, and outdoor furniture. Small BioHavens™, up to about 25sf (2.3m²), are easily moved from one water body to another, however, once installed, the islands should be anchored, so that they maintain their position and do not migrate toward the shoreline.

Manufacturer: Floating Island International

Newspaper Nitrate Treatment

Bioretention is a method for improving the quality of stormwater runoff before it reaches waterways and bodies. Stormwater, having collected surface pollutants from impervious surfaces such as parking lots and roads, is directed into a vegetated bioretention facility. The contaminated stormwater flows through a vegetated layer of engineered soil before it infiltrates or collects in a slotted under-drain, and finally discharges into a nearby stream or water body. The soil and mulch substrate filters and absorbs sediment and heavy metals. The vegetation acts as a filter for sediments and also maintains an active microbial population that can break down chemicals and uptake some excess nutrients.

Some pollutants are more difficult to filter with bioretention. Nitrate, one of the primary nutrient pollutants that contribute to the degradation of water bodies, will travel unabated through a soil matrix. Allen P. Davis's research at the University of Maryland investigates new technological modifications to bioretention to capture and treat nitrate runoff. His work explores microbial denitrification, one of the few natural pathways for treating nitrates. Denitrification organisms convert the nitrate in the water into a harmless nitrogen gas. However, effective denitrification requires an anaerobic (without oxygen) condition with access to a source of carbon.

Interestingly, shredded newspaper, a synthetic waste material, has proven itself as an effective source of carbon for denitrification. In laboratory research Allen Davis found that it performed best in comparison to a number of other organic materials, including straw and sawdust. In order to test its capacity in the field, Davis and his team modified a standard bioretention system. Shredded newspaper is mixed with coarse sand to create a new layer under the soil media. This layer is kept continuously saturated with water by keeping the underdrain elbowed upward, thus maintaining an anaerobic condition. The field test uses a ratio of 17g (0.6oz) of newspaper per 1kg (2.2lbs) of sand. Future measurements and monitoring will determine the effectiveness of this modification in improving the nitrate levels of the adjacent parking lot stormwater discharges.

Research: Allen P. Davis, PhD, Civil and Env. Eng. Director, Maryland Water Resources, University of Maryland

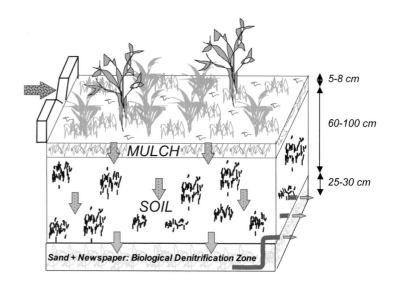

5-8 cm

60-100 cm

25-30 cm

MULCH

SOIL

Sand + Newspaper: Biological Denitrification Zone

Data Fountain

Launch	Stratify	Fluid	Grooming	Digestive	Translate	Volatile

The Data Fountain is a prototype for the translation of real-time relative and comparative information into a fountain. Three fountain jets, placed against a backdrop of different currency symbols, measure the relative values and fluctuations of each currency through the intensity of water flow. Currency data is retrieved from an online source and is updated every 5 sec.

With Data Fountain, Koert van Mensvoort intends to supplant the "noisy screens" typical of information displays with a "calm technology". He asserts that fountains are a source of tranquility and could be a means to rethink how information is displayed within our environment. Datafountain displays are a potentially unobtrusive, even attractive, means of displaying real-time information within a passive environment. While information sources could be any remote source suitable for water displays, the fountain's site invites a relationship between information and context. Certain contextual environmental information, such as stormwater, movement, or transportation, may become particularly meaningful within a datafountain display.

The greatest challenge of the Data Fountain was determining the algorithm for relating the relative values of the currency in a way that would conform to the physical range of the jets and provide a visually intriguing display. The defined algorithm displays the longer-term relative development of currency rates with the more constant height and micro-fluctuations with temporary exaggerated jumps and drops.

Designer: Koert van Mensvoort

Sandscape & Illuminating Clay

Launch	Stratify	Fluid	Grooming	Digestive	**Translate**	Volatile

Sandscape & Illuminating Clay integrates physical model making with real-time computational analysis. Digital and physical representation are placed within an advanced feedback loop, rather than serving as separate stages within the design process. With this technology the designer can rapidly sculpt and explore complex geometries and also have a precise understanding of the systematic and physical consequences of their geo-spatial configuration. Analysis of the physical model can produce representations of forces that change over time, producing numerical data at accuracies that far surpass the tolerances of most physical models.

Users sculpt the topography of a clay/sand landscape model manually while the changing geometry is captured by a ceiling-mounted laser scanner or infrared (IR) light sensing technology. In the computer, the sensing output is transformed into the digital elevation model (DEM) format as well as a series of Geographic Information System (GIS) analysis maps, which are then projected back onto the landscape model. The whole interaction loop happens in near-real-time (approximately one second per cycle).

Elevation is displayed on the model using a color map ranging from red to purple. Volume of cut and fill, water flow, land erosion, view shed and solar aspect is also calculated and displayed in real time. Two cross sections are projected beside the model to describe the 3-D geometry of the terrain. A vertical screen or an LCD screen displays a 3-D perspective view of the landscape.

Illuminating Clay uses a modified commercially available laser scanner, calibrated with a video projector. The scanner/projector pair is housed inside an aluminum casing at a height of 2m (6.6ft) above the surface of the modeling material. Scanned data is re-sampled into x, y, z coordinates and then converted into GIS format.

Sandscape uses a more affordable sensing technology, which includes a box containing 1mm diameter glass beads lit from beneath with an array of 600 high-power IR light emitting diodes (LED). An infrared camera is mounted 2m (6.6ft) above the surface of the beads and captures the intensity of light passing through the volume. The intensity of transmitted light is a function of the depth of the beads and a look-up table can be used to convert surface radiance values into surface elevation values.

R&D: SENSEable City Laboratory, Tangible Media Group, MIT
Researchers: Hiroshi Ishii, Carlo Ratti, Ben Piper, Yao Wang, Assaf Biderman and Eran Ben-Joseph

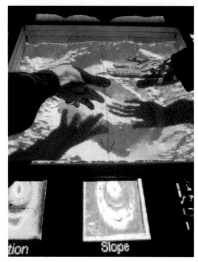

Outdoor Misting Systems

Launch	Stratify	Fluid	Grooming	Digestive	Translate	Volatile

Fogco's Outdoor Misting Systems produce water mist and fog for a range of applications ranging from temperature control, insect repelling, and suppression of dust particles, to ambient visual effects. The system creates mist using high-pressure water pumps that force water up to 1,000psi (6 894, kPa) through tiny nozzles, converting a stream of water into droplets as small as 5mic. At this size the atomized droplets can undergo "flash evaporation", drawing heat from the environment and reducing ambient temperature by up to 40°F (4.4°C) depending on the relative humidity.

As a cooling system, water mist can be employed in any number of configurations to affect localized temperature. It can be integrated with a fan system to produce microclimates. As a humidification system, misters can maintain an ideal moisture content level, such as for greenhouse applications, as well as reduce static electricity.

Outdoor Misting Systems can also be employed to suppress dust, odor, and insects. A Fogco System can produce a high concentration of 10mic fog droplets that are the optimum size for the attraction and suppression of dust particles, ranging in size from 0.1–1000mic. Fog systems can eliminate odors associated with solid waste treatment facilities, microbial decomposition of animal waste, and noxious volatile compounds. Some of the more common problems include carbon dioxide, ammonia, hydrogen sulfide, and methane. And although odorless, carbon dioxide and methane can be lethal. Fog system applications for odor suppression include: chemical plants, solid waste and waste transfer stations, construction sites, landfills, composting facilities, etc.

Mixing the mist water source with a natural insecticide, such as Pyrethrum, an extract from the Chrysanthemum flower, can repel insects, including mosquitoes.

The misting systems are also utilized to create ambient visual effects. Misting nozzles embedded in the surround of a pool can create the dramatic visual effect of fog rolling over water. Fog can be used for many configurations integrated with lighting to create, for example, a rainbow effect.

Manufacturer: Fogco Systems, Inc.

Project credits

Launch

Multi-Tiered Vine Park

Project	MFO Park
Location	Zurich, Switzerland
Client	Grün Stadt Zürich
Design	Raderschall Landschaftsarchitekten AG, Meilen, Switzerland, www.raderschall.ch
General Planners	Planergemeinschaft MFO-Park, Burckhardt + Partner AG
Structural Engineers	Basler und Hofmann, Zurich, Switzerland
Furniture Design	Frédéric Dedeley, Zurich, Switzerland
Year	competition 1998, construction 2001–2002, opening 2003

Misting Vine Pergola

Project	Parque de Diagonal Mar
Location	Barcelona, Spain
Architects	Enric Miralles Benedetta Tagliabue, EMBT Arquitectes Associates, www.mirallestagliabue.com
Design Team	Elena Rocchi, Lluis Cabtallops, Fabiaán Asunción
Urban Planning Architects	Oscar Tusquets, Xavier Sust
Engineers	Europroject Consultores Asociados, José María Velasco
Construction	Benjumea
Year	1997– 2002

Wind Adapted Road Canopy Structure

Project	Palio de Bougainvilleas
Location	Avenida Roosevelt, San Juan, Puerto Rico
Client	DTOP – Departamento de Transportaciòn y Obras Públicas San Juan
Design	West 8, Rotterdam, Holland, www.west8.nl
Design Team	Adriaan Geuze, Edzo Bindels, Jerry van Eyck, Cyrus B. Clark, Sander Lap, Juan Sánchez Muñoz, Anna Holder, Carlos Peña,
Year	2004 – ongoing

Fire-Escape Ecosystem

Project	Vertical Garden
Location	Fair Street Housing, London, U.K.
Client	Fair Street Housing
Design	GROSS.MAX (Landscape Architects) Edinburgh, U.K. www. grossmax.com + Mark Dion (artist) PA, USA
Art Management	Isabel Vaseur / Vicky Lewis of Art Office London
Year	scheduled 2007

Parasitic Vegetal Structure

Project	MAK t6 VACANT
Location	The MAK Center and SCI-Arc, Los Angeles, CA, USA
Client	The MAK Center and SCI-Arc
Design	David Fletcher + Juan Azulay
Year	competition 2006

Stratify

Mechanically Stabilized Landform

Project	Olympic Sculpture Park
Location	Seattle Art Museum, Seattle, WA, USA
Client	Seattle Art Museum
Design	Weiss/Manfredi Architects, New York, NY, USA
Design team	Marion Weiss and Michael A. Manfredi (Design Partners), Christopher Ballentine (Project Manager), Todd Hoehn and Yehre Suh (Project Architects), Michael Blasberg, Emily Clanahan, Lauren Crahan, Kok Kian Goh, Hamilton Hadden, Mike Harshman, Mustapha Jundi, Justin Kwok, John Peek, Akari Takebayashi
Structural and Civil Engineering Consultant	Magnusson Klemencic Associates
Landscape Architect Consultant	Charles Anderson Landscape Architect
Art Program Coordinator	Owen Richards Architects

Mechanical and Electrical Engineering	ABACUS Engineered Systems
Lighting Design Consultant	Brandston Partnership Inc.
Geotechnical Engineering Consultant	Hart Crowser
Environmental Consultant	Aspect Consulting
Aquatic Engineering Consultant	Anchor Environmental
Graphics Consultant	Pentagram
Security and AV/IT	ARUP
Project Management	Barrientos LLC
Contractor	Sellen Construction
Year	2006

Floating Grass Plain

Project	Wonder Holland
Location	Rome, Italy
Client	Dutch Embassy, Mercati di Traiano
Design	West 8, Rotterdam, Holland, www.west8.nl
Design Team	Adriaan Geuze, Edzo Bindels, Rob van 't Hof, Riëtte Bosch, Freek Boerwinkel, Adriana Mueller
Year	2004

Multi-Operational Modular Surface

Project	The High Line, Section I
Location	High Line, New York, NY, USA
Design	Field Operation, New York, NY, USA, www.fieldoperations.net
Design Team	James Corner, Tom Jost, Lisa Switkin, Nahyun Hwang, Maura Rockcastle
Architects	Diller Scofidio + Renfro
Planting Design	Piet Oudolf

Gradient of Resilience

Project	Safe Zone
Location	7th International Garden Festival, Reford Gardens, Grand-Métis, Quebec, Canada
Landscape Architects	StoSS Landscape Urbanism, Boston, MA, USA, www.stoss.net
Design Team	Chris Reed (principal) Chris Muskopf, Tim Barner, Scott Bishop, Kristin Malone, Graham Palmer, Karyn Williams
Material Donors	Yellow Alert Mats by Cape Fear Systems, www.alertmat.com, Black recycled rubber base by SolPlast Inc., www.solplastics.com
Material Discounters	Black recycled SBR surfacing by Recovery Technologies, Canada Inc.; Yellow EPDM by U.S. Rubber Recycling, Inc. www.usrubber.com; Urethane Binder & technical assistance by Sof Surfaces Inc., www.sofsurfaces.com
Installation	Jim Knowles & Paul Wellington, Chunk Rubber, Sof Solutions

Surface Inversion

Project	Maritime Youth House
Location	Sundby Harbour, Copenhagen, Denmark
Client	Kvarterløft Governmental, City Renewal Project, The Space and Facility Foundation for Sports, The Urban Development Fund, Copenhagen
Design	PLOT=BIG+JDS, Copenhagen, Denmark, www.plot.dk
Year	invited competition, 1st prize, completed 2004

Fluid

Weaving Porous and Nonporous Surfaces

Project	Allianz Arena Munich Stadium
Location	Munich, Germany
Client	Allianz Arena München Stadion GmbH, FC Bayern München AG, TSV München von 1860 GmbH & Co. KG
Landscape Architect	Vogt Landschaftsarchitekten Architects, Zurich, Switzerland, www.vogt-la.ch
Architecture	Herzog & de Meuron, Basel, Switzerland
Year	2001–2005

Inflatable Dam System

Project	Environmental Restoration of Besòs River
Location	Barcelona, Spain
Client	Municipality of Barcelona, Municipality of Santa Coloma de Gramenet, Municipality of Montcada i Reixac, Municipality of Sant Adrià de Besòs, The Mancomunitat de Municipis de l'Àrea Metropolitana de Barcelona
Design	Barcelona Regional Agència Metropolitana de Desenvolupament Urbanístic i d'Infraestructures S.A., Barcelona, Spain
Year	1997– 2000, 2002 – 2004

Stormwater Garden

Project	Blackstone Power Plant Renovation
Location	Harvard University, Cambridge, MA, USA
Client	Harvard University Operations Services
Design	Landworks Studio, Inc. Boston, MA, USA, www.landworks-studio.com
Design team	Michael Blier (Principal), Tim Baird (Senior Landscape Architect), Letitia Tormay (Project Manager)
Architect	Bruner/Cott, Cambridge, MA, USA
Soil Scientist	Tim Craul, Craul Land Scientists
Civil Engineer	Green International
Year	2006

Drop Structures for Suburban Stormwater System

Project	Shop Creek
Location	Aurora, CO, USA
Client	City of Aurora, Colorado
Design	Wenk Associates, Inc. Denver, CO, USA www.wenkla.com
Architect	Black & Veatch
Engineer	Mueller Engineering, Inc.
Year	1988 – 1989

Networked Sidewalk Stormwater System

Project	SW 12th Avenue Green Street Project
Location	Portland, OR, USA
Client	City of Portland, Oregon
Design	Portland Bureau of Environmental Services, www.portlandon-line.com/BES/
Year	2005

Biotechnical Wave & Erosion Control Structures

Project	The Delta In-Channel Island Work Group, CALFED Project # 2001-E200
Location	Sacramento-San Joaquin River, San Francisco Bay, CA, USA
Government Agencies	San Francisco Estuary Project and Association of Bay Area Governments, CALFED Bay Delta Authority, Delta Protection Commission, Department of Fish and Game, Department of Water, State Lands Commission, US Fish and Wildlife Service
Engineering Design, Prime Design Contractors	MBK Engineers
Construction Cost Estimator	DCC Engineering
Environmental Documentation	EIP Associates
Biotechnical Contractor	Hart Inc.
Biologist	Kjeldsen Biological Consulting
Survey Contractor, Topographic/Bathmetry	KSN Engineers
Biotechnical Design	Andrew Leiser, PhD, Professor Emeritus UC Davis
Biological Monitoring	LFR Levine-Fricke
Biotechnical Design, Monitoring	LSA Associates Inc.
Hydrodynamic Surveys & Monitoring	Swanson Hydrology and Geomorphology
Year	2001 – 2006

Grooming

Tree Crutches Growing Guides

Project	Courtyard Garden, University Library
Location	Universiteit Utrecht, Utrecht, Holland
Client	Universiteit Utrecht
Design	West 8, Rotterdam, Holland, www.west8.nl
Design Team	Adriaan Geuze, Martin Biewenga, Joost Koningen
Year	scheduled completion 2005

Hedge-Trimming Armature

Project	The Lurie Garden
Location	Millennium Park, Chicago, IL, USA
Client	Millennium Park, Inc.
Design	Gustafson Guthrie Nichol, Seattle, WA, USA, www.ggnltd.com
Plant Design	Piet Oudolf, Robert Israel
Engineers	KPFF
Fountain Consultants	CMS Collaborative
Year	completion 2004

Artificial Winter Climate for a Bamboo Garden

Project	Hybridized Hydrologies
Location	Erie Street Plaza, Milwaukee, WI, USA
Landscape architects	StoSS Landscape Urbanism, Boston, MA, USA, www.stoss.net
Design Team	Chris Reed (principal), Tim Barner, Scott Bishop, Kristin Malone, Chris Muskopf, Graham Palmer
Urban Design	Vetter Denk Architecture, Milwaukee, WI, USA
Engineering and Infrastructure	Graef Anhalt Schloemer & Associates, Milwaukee, WI, USA
Lighting Design	Light Th!s, Boston, MA, USA
Year	competition winning entry, scheduled completion 2007

Saltwater Herbicide System

Project	Marsh Planters
Location	East River Ferry Landings, New York, NY, USA
Design	Ken Smith Landscape Architect, New York, NY, USA
Design Team	Tobias Arnborst, Elizabeth Asawa, Heike Begdolt, Yoonchul Cho, Alex Felson, Ruth Hartmann, Rocio Lastras Montana, Ken Smith, Dan Willner
Architect	Kennedy & Violich Architecture, Boston, MA, USA
Marine/Structural Engineers	M.G. McLaren, P.C.
Construction Managers	Hudson Meridian Construction Group
M/E/P	Lakhani & Jordan Engineering
Security	Cosentini Associates
Riparian Wetland and Habitat Experts	Carl Alderson, Parks Dept., Natural Resources Group; Dr. Michael Levandowsky, Marine Microbiologists at Pace University; Steve Zahn, Department of Environmental Conservation Bureau of Marine Resources; Robbin Bergfors, NYC Parks Department; Sue Mcinich, horticulturalist, Pinelands Nursery; Leslie Hunter, Environmental Concerns in Maryland; Edward Toth, Greenbelt Native Plant Center on Staten Island
Year	concept 2001

Low-Maintenance Perennial Plantings

Project	Riemer Park Perennial Meadows
Location	Messestadt Riem, Munich, Germany
Client	Landeshauptstadt München, Baureferat HA Gartenbau
represented by	MRG Maßnahmeträger München - Riem GmbH
Planning & Design	LUZ Landschaftsarchitekten München, www.heiner-luz.de
Design Team	Heiner Luz, Sibylle Kraft, Roland Großberger
Park Planning	Latitude Nord, Gilles Vexlard, Laurence Vacherot, David Schulz, Philip Denkinger
Year	1998 – 2005

Stunted Growth Pattern

Project	Elsässertor office building
Location	Basel, Switzerland
Client	ARGE Generalplaner Elsässertor, Geschäftshaus Elsässertor
Landscape Architect	Vogt Landschaftsarchitekten, Zurich, Switzerland, www.vogt-la.ch/
Architecture	Herzog & de Meuron, Basel, Switzerland
Year	2003 – 2005

Digestive

Bio-Remediation Park Design

Project	Former British Petroleum Park
Location	Sydney, Australia
Client	North Sydney Council
Design	McGregor+Partners, Sydney, Australia, www.mcgregorpartners.com.au
Civil & Structural Engineering	Northrop
Geo Tech	Jeffery and Katauskas
Heritage	Sue Rosen & Associates
Signage	Wishart Design
Soil Specialists	Sydney Environmental and Soil Laboratory
Certifiers	DLM Consulting
Quantity surveyors	Milliken Berson Madden
Surveying	PSN Surveying
Builder	BT Contractors
Year	2003 – 2005

Fluvially Integrated Effluent Wetlands

Project	Environmental Restoration of Besòs River
Location	Barcelona, Spain
Client	Municipality of Barcelona, Municipality of Santa Coloma de Gramenet, Municipality of Montcada i Reixac, Municipality of Sant Adrià de Besòs, The Mancomunitat de Municipis de l'Àrea Metropolitana de Barcelona
Design	Barcelona Regional Agència Metropolitana de Desenvolupament Urbanístic i d'Infraestructures S.A., Barcelona, Spain
Year	1997– 2000, 2002 – 2004

Water-Cleansing Biotope

Project	DaimlerChrysler Immobilien AG
Location	Potsdamer Platz, Berlin, Germany
Client	DaimlerChrysler Immobilien AG, Karl-Heinz Bohn
Landscape Architect	Atelier Dreiseitl, Überlingen, Germany, www.dreiseitl.de
Design Team	Herbert Dreiseitl, Andreas Bockemühl, Klaus Schroll, Alexander Edel, Gerhard Hauber, Christoph Hald
Substrate Material Research	Technical University of Berlin, Germany: Marco Schmidt, Katharina Teschner
Year	1999

On-Site Sewage Treatment System

Project	Sidwell Friends School
Location	Washington, D.C., USA
Client	Sidwell Friends School, Washington, D.C.
Landscape Architect	Andropogon Associates, Ltd., Philadelphia, PA, USA, www.andropogon.com
Architect	Kieran Timberlake Associates, LLP
Wastewater Engineer	Natural Systems International
MEP/FP Engineer	Bruce Brooks & Associates
Structural Engineer	CVM Engineers
Civil Engineer	VIKA Inc.
Lighting Consultants	Sean O'Connor Associates Lighting Consultants Inc.; Benya Lighting Design

LEED Consultant	Green Shape LLC; Integrative Design Collaborative
Owner's Representative	JFW, Inc.
General Contractor	Hitt Contracting
Year	2006 – ongoing

Ground Reconstitution Strategy

Project	How to Barney Rubble
Location	Urban Outfitters Navy Yard Headquarters, Philadelphia, PA, USA
Industrial Site Architect	D.I.R.T. studio, Charlottesville, VA, USA, www.dirtstudio.com
Design Team	Julie Bargmann (Founding Principal), Chris Fannin (Managing Partner), David Hill (Associate)
Architect	MS&R Architects, Minneapolis, MN, USA
Civil & Landscape Architect	Gladnick Wright Salameda, West Chester, PA, USA
Landscape Contractor	Turning Leaf, Langhorn, PA, USA
Year	compled 2006

Strategic Contaminated Soil Placement

Project	Cultuurpark Westergasfabriek
Location	Amsterdam, Holland
Client	Evert Verhagen, Projectbureau Westergasfabriek, Westerpark District Council and City of Amsterdam
Landscape Architects	Gustafson Porter, London, U.K., www.gustafson-porter.com
Design Team	Kathryn Gustafson, Neil Porter, Neil Black, Juanita Cheung, Frances Kristie, Philippe Marchand, Gerben Mienis, Rachel Mooney, Mieke Tanghe, Pauline Wieringa
Architect	Francine Houben, Mecanoo
Concept Design Engineer	Arup
Structural Engineer	Arup
Construction Engineer	Pieters Bouwtechniek
Construction Engineer	Rene Vilijn, Tauw
Design Project Management	Northcroft Belgium
Construction Project Management	Rene Vilijn, Tauw

General Contractor	Marcus bv
Year	completed 2004

Translate

Pneumatic Body

Project	Pneumatic Body, Ephemeral Structures
Location	Olympic Games, Athens, Greece
Design	ONL [Oosterhuis_Lénárd], Rotterdam, Holland, www.oosterhuis.nl
Design Team	Kas Oosterhuis, Stephan Gustin, Titusz Tarnai, Ines Moreira
Year	concept 2002

Powered by Wind, the Ground is a Turntable

Project	Courtyard In the Wind
Location	Buildings Department Administration Building, Munich, Germany
Client	Buildings Department Administration Building, München
Design	Acconci Studio, New York, NY, USA, www.acconci.com
Design Team	Vito Acconci, Dario Nunez, Celia Imrey, Saija Singer, Luis Vera, Sergio Prego
Landscape Architect	Wolfgang Hermann Niemeyer, Munich, Germany
Year	1997– 2000

Weather Informed Park Access System

Project	Environmental Restoration of Besòs River
Location	Barcelona, Spain
Client	Municipality of Barcelona, Municipality of Santa Coloma de Gramenet, Municipality of Montcada i Reixac, Municipality of Sant Adrià de Besòs, The Mancomunitat de Municipis de l'Àrea Metropolitana de Barcelona
Design	Barcelona Regional Agència Metropolitana de Desenvolupament Urbanístic i d'Infraestructures S.A., Barcelona, Spain
Year	1997– 2000, 2002 – 2004

Fiber Optic Marsh

Project	Field's Point
Location	Providence, RI, USA
Design	Abby Feldman, Brooklyn, NY, USA
Year	concept 2003, Harvard University, Graduate School of Design

Volatile

Responsive Cloud Machine

Project	Harvey Milk Memorial
Location	San Francisco, CA, USA
Client	Harvey Milk Memorial competition, City of San Francisco, California
Design	Christian Werthmann & LOMA architecture.landscape.urbanism
Design Team	Christian Werthmann, Petra Brunnhofer, Wolfgang Schück, Ilija Vukorep
Year	winning competition entry, 2000

Computer Animated Rain

Project	Pitterpattern
Location	Scharnhauser Park, Stuttgart, Germany
Client	Stadt.haus, Stuttgart
Design Team	J. MAYER H. Architekten, Berlin, Germany, www.jmayerh.de + Sebastian Finckh
Project Architects	Andre Santer, Sebastian Finckh
Architect on site	Architekturbüro Uli Wiesler, Stuttgart, Germany
Year	1999

Dynamic Thermal Wind Wall

Project	Fragmented Dunes + Fragmented Sea
Location	Mesa Arts Center, Mesa, AZ, USA
Client	Mesa Arts Center
Design	Ned Kahn, www.nedkahn.com/
Architects	BOORA and DWL Architects
Engineering	Paragon
Year	2005

Project	Technorama Façade
Location	Technorama, Winterthur, Switzerland
Client	Technorama
Design	Ned Kahn, www.nedkahn.com/
Architects	Dürig & Rämi Architekten
Year	2002

Impression of Rain

Project	Weather Garden
Location	The Park Hyatt Hotel, Zurich, Switzerland
Client	Park Hyatt, Zürich, Hyatt International, EAME Ltd.
Landscape Architect	Vogt Landschaftsarchitekten, Zurich, Switzerland, www.vogt-la.ch/
Architecture	Meili, Peter Architekten, Zurich, Switzerland
Year	2002 – 2004

Acknowlegements

We would like to extend special thanks to Niall Kirkwood, chair of the Landscape Architecture Department at Harvard Graduate School of Design (GSD), and George Beylerian, president and founder of Material ConneXion, for their professional and intellectual support.

This book would have not been possible without the assistance of many, especially Darlene Montgomery for her valuable insight and editorial assistance; Hugh Wilburn, director of GSD Loeb Library & Materials Collection; Beatrice Saraga, Zaneta Hong, GSD Materials Collection researchers; Toshiko Mori, chair of the Architecture Department, GSD; and the many firms and individuals who contributed content.

We would also like to thank our friends, family, and respective employers, Hargreaves Associates and Mia Lehrer + Associates, for their great support during this endeavor.

The Graham Foundation generously provided grant support for this publication.

Illustration credits

Page numbers refer to captions

Acconci Studio: 128, 129
Acrayfish Alex Kotlov: 166
Andropogon Associates, Ltd.: 112, 113
Arup: 119, 120 (2 and 4), 121 (6)
Atelier Dreiseitl: 111
Barcelona Regional, Agència Metropolitana de Desenvolupament Urbanístic i d'Infraestructures S.A.: 62, 63, 106, 107, 108, 109, 130, 131
Benjamin Benschneider: 39 (1)
Hélène Binet: 121 (5 right)
BioHaven™ Wild Floating Islands: 172, 173
Brett Boardman: 102, 105 (4)
Bridgestone Industrial Products America, Inc.: 163
Thomas Burla: 20 (1)
Cahill Associates: 160 top right, middle and bottom
Brett Cornish: 103 (2), 105 (5)
Benjamin Davidson: 165 bottom
Allen P. Davis: 174
D.I.R.T. studio: 114, 115, 116, 117
Enric Miralles Benedetta Tagliabue, EMBT Architects Associates: 23

Rob Feenstra: 120 (1)
Abby Feldman: cover, 132, 133
Field Operations with Diller Scofidio + Renfro. Courtesy of the City of New York: 44, 45, 46
David Fletcher + Juan Azulay: 34, 35
David Franck: 138
Freecell: 151
Fogco Systems, Inc.: 177
Alex Gaultier, courtesy of Enric Miralles Benedetta Tagliabue, EMBT Architects Associates: 22, 24, 25
Geoproducts: 155
GROSS.MAX + Mark Dion: 30, 31, 32, 33
G-SKY, Inc.: 150
Gustafson Guthrie Nichol: 80, 81, 82, 83
Mads Hilmer: 53 (4), 54 (2), 55
Illustrating Light, Inta Eihmane: 167 top left
Anita Kahn Photography, Cambridge, MA: 152, 153, 154, 159, 160 top left, 162, 164
Ned Kahn: 142 (2), 143 (1), 144, 145
Landworks Studio, Inc.: 64, 65, 66, 67
T. Lindenbaum (Photography): 165 top
LUZ Landschaftsarchitekten: 92, 93, 94, 95

Magnusson Klemencic Associates: 41 1st right

Liat Margolis: 176

J. MAYER H.: 140

McGregor+Partners: 103 (3), 105 (3)

Koert van Mensvoort: 175

Bruce C Moore: 40 1st right

Richard Nichols, LSA Associates, Inc. and Chris Kjeldsen, Kjeldsen Biological Consulting: 72, 73, 74, 75

ONL [oosterhuis_lénárd]: 124, 125, 126, 127

PATTERNS / Marcelo Spina: 156, 157

PLOT=BIG+JDS: 52, 53 (3), 54 (1)

Portland Bureau of Environmental Services: 70, 71

Portland Cement Association: 161, 171

Profile Products LLC, Mat, Inc.: 152 bottom

raderschall landschaftsarchitekten ag: 17, 18, 20 (2), 21

Shawn Roberts, Sparklingmoments: 167 right

Alexander Robinson: 121 (5 left)

Petronella Ryan: 104 (1)

Nina Sabbuk, Urban Horticulture Institute, Department of Horticulture, Cornell University: 158

Christiane Seiler (Photography): 99 (4)

Ken Smith Landscape Architect: 88, 89, 90, 91

StoSS Landscape Urbanism: 48, 49, 50, 51, 84, 85, 86, 87

Technorama, The Swiss Science Center: 142 (1)

TK Edens: 167 bottom left

The University of Guelph-Humber Living Wall. Diamond and Schmitt Architects, Inc. and RHL in joint partnership. Living wall by Air Quality Solutions Ltd.: 170

Olaf Unverzart (Photography): 59, 60, 61

Vogt Landschaftsarchitekten: 58, 59, 60, 61, 96, 97, 98, 99 (3 and 5), 146, 147

Weiss/Manfredi: 39 (2, 3), 40 left (all drawings), 40 2nd right, 40 3rd right, 40 4th right, 41 left (all drawings), 41 2nd right, 41 3rd right

Wenk Associates, Inc.: 68, 69

Christian Werthmann & LOMA: 136, 137

West 8: 26, 28, 29, 42, 43, 78, 79

Westergasfabriek Park: 120 (3)

Western Ecology, LLC: 168, 169

Simon Wood: 104 (2)

Index

atmosphere	climate	contol	16, 22, 26, 58, 84, 136, 138, 142, 170, 177
energy	fire	control	163, 165
	kinetic	motion	62, 124, 128, 142, 163
	light	emit	130, 132, 136, 176
		reflect	142, 146
		shade	16, 142
	solar	power	132, 172
	sound	sense	124, 175
flow	air	circulate	170, 172
		filter/biofilter	30, 150, 170, 177
		inflate	62, 163
		pneumatic	62, 124, 163
		remediate	170, 171, 177
	data	interact	124, 136, 138
		model	175, 176
		sense	62, 84, 88, 124, 130, 132, 136, 163, 175, 176
		signal	124, 128, 130, 132, 136, 138, 175, 176
	vapor	cloud	136, 138, 177
		fog	136, 177
		mist	22, 136, 177
		steam	84
	water	absorb	58, 70, 88 151, 152, 153, 158, 160, 162, 174
		aerobic	68, 70, 104, 112
		anaerobic	112, 174
		circulate	16, 22, 44, 58, 110, 112, 138, 175
		dissipate/attenuate	68, 72
		evaporate	146

flow	water	filter/biofilter	64, 68, 70, 104, 106, 110, 112, 172, 174
		generate, rain	138
		infiltrate	58, 64, 70, 112, 152, 153, 158, 158, 160
		irrigate	16, 22, 30, 34, 44, 58, 64, 70, 88, 106, 112
		porous, non/impervious	58, 68, 118, 161, 163
		porous/pervious/permeable	48, 58, 64, 70, 110, 114, 150, 151, 152, 153, 154, 158, 160, 162, 164, 170, 172, 174
		prevent, eutrophication	64, 68, 70, 104, 106, 110, 112, 172, 174
		prevent, flood	22, 62, 62, 64, 68, 70, 72, 106, 160, 162, 163
		register, rain	146
		retain	58, 62, 64, 68, 110, 146, 163, 174
		reuse	16, 85, 104, 112, 138
		treat, effluent	106, 112
		treat, stormwater	58, 64, 68, 70, 104, 110, 112, 138, 174
	wind	adapt	26
		power	128, 172
		register	128, 142
		resist	16, 26, 80, 168
growth	fungal	mycoremediate	166
	fungal/vegetation	biodegrade	64, 70, 104, 106, 110, 112, 166, 170, 172, 174
	vegetation	fungal, anti	92
		gradient	30, 44, 88, 172
		seed	151, 152, 153, 165, 168
		self-propagate	92, 172
		shade	16, 22, 26, 30, 34
		shape/manipulate	78, 80
		stabilize	38, 72, 152, 153, 154, 156, 161
		successional	92, 165

growth	vegetation	support/reinforce	16, 22, 26, 30, 34, 78, 150, 151, 152, 153, 154, 156, 158, 170, 172
		suppress/inhibit	78, 88, 92, 96, 159, 164, 165
matter/systems	chemical	photocatalyze	171
	soil	cap	118
		move/ cut & fill	118
		remediate/ decontaminate	104, 118, 166
		resist, compaction	154, 158, 159
		sediment/deposit	64, 68, 70, 72, 106
		stabilize	38, 68, 72, 132, 151, 152, 153, 154, 156, 158, 161
		biodegradable	72, 132, 151, 152, 153, 162, 172, 174
		composite/reconstitute	48, 64, 114, 118, 158
		control, erosion	38, 68, 72, 132, 152, 153, 154, 156
		elevated/suspended	16, 22, 26, 30, 34, 42, 44, 52, 58, 88, 150, 151, 170
		flexible/resilient/elastomeric	48, 62, 124, 151, 152, 153, 154, 159, 162, 163, 164
		float	72, 172
		fungal, anti	48, 159
		layered	42, 44, 48, 58, 64, 68, 106, 110, 114, 118, 150, 158, 170, 174
		load-bearing	38, 34, 38, 42, 44, 48, 52, 58, 114, 118, 128, 146 154, 158, 159, 160, 161, 172
		modular	30, 38, 44, 52, 80, 88, 142, 150, 156, 156
		multi-tiered	16, 30, 34, 38, 150, 151 170
		network/distribute	16, 62, 68, 70, 106, 124, 130, 138, 175
		reactive/responsive	62, 84, 88, 124, 128, 130, 132, 136, 138, 142 163, 171, 175, 176
		reuse/recycle	30, 34, 48, 68, 72, 104, 114, 118, 159, 161, 174
		support/reinforce	78, 80, 152, 153, 154, 156, 158
		tensile	16, 26, 34, 124

On the authors

Liat Margolis was Director of Material Research at Material ConneXion, an innovative multi-industry materials research and consulting company. Recently she helped develop the Materials Collection at Harvard's Graduate School of Design and won the Harvard University's Presidential Instructional Technology Fellows Program award for her work within the Collection. She has taught materials innovation and environmental issues within the Product Design and Architecture departments at Parsons The New School for Design and has published in many design magazines, including Dwell, I.D. and Ottagono.

Liat earned her BA in Industrial Design from Rhode Island School of Design (RISD) and her Masters of Landscape Architecture from Harvard's Graduate School of Design. She currently divides her time between consulting for the GSD's Materials Collection conducting further research, and practicing at Hargreaves Associates as the project manager of the Knoxville South Waterfront Master Plan. Liat, originally from Israel, currently works and lives in Cambridge, MA.

Alexander Robinson has helped lead numerous urban landscape technology and planning research projects with Harvard's Center for Technology and Environment. Alexander was part of a GSD student collaborative that was featured in the 2nd International Architecture Biennale Rotterdam: The Flood. He was also part of a student group that received the ASLA honor award for a landscape-planning project titled Alternative Futures for Tepotzotlán, Mexico.

Alexander studied fine arts and computer science at Swarthmore College and earned his Masters in Landscape Architecture from Harvard's Graduate School of Design. While working at Mia Lehrer + Associates, he helped author the Los Angeles River and Compton Creek Master Plans. Alexander currently works and lives in Los Angeles, CA.

They are both recipients of a grant from the Graham Foundation to assist in the research and development of this publication.

Liat and Alexander began their collaboration while attending the Harvard Graduate School of Design Landscape Architecture program. They have plans to continue their collaboration and further expand and promote the topics covered in this book. They can be contacted via the website www.livingsystemsLA.com.